DEPTH
OVER TIME

DEPTH OVER TIME

KUNDALINI SADHANA:
A PATH OF TRANSFORMATION
AND LIBERATION

SWAMI KHECARANATHA

With a Preface by Mark Dyczkowski, Ph.D.

ISBN-13: 978-1496101532

ISBN-10: 978-1496101537

First published by AuthorHouse 10/08/2010

Library of Congress Control Number: 2010913389

Printed in the United States of America

Swami Khecaranatha's books are published under his own imprint, Prasad Press.

ALSO BY SWAMI KHECARANATHA

Merging With the Divine: One Day at a Time (2011)

The Heart of Recognition: The Wisdom & Practices of the Pratyabhijna Hrdayam (2013)

Shiva's Trident: The Consciousness of Freedom and the Means to Liberation (2013)

Wearing God's Mala: The Seva Sutras (forthcoming in 2014)

DEDICATION

I dedicate this book to my students, my teachers,
and to the God that is always present, already
within each of us.

ACKNOWLEDGMENTS

This book is the result of the work of a team of people whose many talents have brought it to published form. I am grateful for their assistance and wish to extend my thanks to all of them.

Breda Boran-Sears diligently performed the arduous task of transcribing many of the talks from my retreats to create a raw manuscript.

Ellen Jefferds took on the massive and daunting task of integrating all of those transcripts into a cohesive body of material. Without her one-pointed effort it would not have been possible for this book to be published.

Sonia Foscoli (my life partner), Sassi LaMuth, and Dana Swain volunteered to be readers of the manuscript and provided invaluable feedback that helped bring clarity and flow to the content.

Christine Sheridan did a meticulous job of copyediting the final manuscript.

Keith Jefferds assisted in creating the graphics.

Mark Dyczkowski wrote an eloquent preface that succinctly describes the relationship of my practice to the tradition of Kashmir Shaivism.

CONTENTS

Editor's Note   xiii

Preface by Mark Dyczkowski   xvii

From the Author, About His Lineage   xxvii

BOOK ONE

The Secret Teaching   1

BOOK TWO

Introduction: Depth Over Time   11

SECTION ONE

LIBERATION: THE EXPERIENCE OF ONENESS

1. God Is One, Without a Second   21

2. Freedom in This Lifetime   37

3. *Kuṇḍalinī Sādhana:* A Path to Liberation   53

SECTION TWO

CONSCIOUS STUDENTSHIP: THE SADHANA OF TRANSFORMATION

4. The Fire of Consciousness   93

5. The Wish to Grow   119

6. The Relationship With an Authentic Teacher   133

7. The Alchemy of Selfless Service   159

8. Conscious Choice & Disciplined Action   179

9. Surrender: The Doorway Into the Divine   205

10. Living in the Heart of Stillness   241

Pronunciation Guide   266

EDITOR'S NOTE

When Swami Khecaranatha (Nathaji) asked me to serve as the editor of this book, my immediate reaction was to feel quite honored by his request. I had been a student at Sacred Space Yoga Sanctuary for only eighteen months, and actively involved as a volunteer for just about a year. Although I was happy to take on the project, my initial response was tempered by a feeling of trepidation. I had previously worked as an editor for a magazine, but my responsibilities had been limited to pieces of about fifteen hundred words. Tackling an entire book would be a very different thing.

I knew that editing this book would be a huge job because the intent was to organize and pare down transcriptions from several years' worth of retreat talks into a coherent stream of knowledge. That in itself was a challenge, because there are several themes that repeat themselves throughout Nathaji's talks, and it was necessary to decide when a repetition provided an opportunity to revisit a topic from another angle, and when it was simply redundant. There are many words, phrases, and topics that do reappear throughout the book, and hopefully the reader will find that such repetition offers new insight into previously discussed subjects.

In addition to organizing the texts and creating a sense of flow from one idea to the next, I had to take material that was delivered orally and translate it into print form. Nathaji is a very warm, colorful speaker who uses a lot of humor and body language, so it's difficult to convey the liveliness of his presence on the printed page. Despite this inherent problem, my goal was to preserve his "voice" as much as possible, even while adapting the text and applying written rules of grammar. One change I did make throughout the book was to use the male pronoun "He" for God (except when specifically referring to the Goddess) and "he" for both teacher and student. It made my job much easier to simplify the wording in this way, and I also think that—if one can allow some flexibility within the feminist viewpoint—it makes reading easier as well.

I agreed to serve as editor because I care very much about this practice and would like to see Swami Khecaranatha gain the recognition he deserves as a spiritual guide. He has been teaching *Kuṇḍalinī sādhana* for nearly forty years (and the head of his own center since 2001), but this is his first book. Those of us who are fortunate to be Nathaji's students know him to be a unique individual—a man of the highest integrity who embodies what he teaches, moment by moment. Nathaji shows us that it is possible to live fully in the world while developing and maintaining our conscious connection with the Divinity within. In fact, he teaches that there is no separation between spiritual life and life in the world.

Nathaji talks in terms that students can understand, and he does so within the context of the challenges of daily living. Although he often discusses Tantric philosophy, and is an inspiring speaker, one of his greatest strengths is being able to speak the language of the streets. He can tune in to people and help them wherever they might feel stuck—whether in their personal relationships, on the job, or with the practice of meditation itself. Nathaji has the ability to translate the highest Tantric teachings into concepts and techniques that Westerners can use as they confront their everyday tensions and the perceived limitations of their lives.

I have certainly found Nathaji's guidance invaluable in my own life. Prior to becoming his student, I had been a teacher of a well-known meditation program for more than thirty years. All roads may lead to Rome, but I can say without hesitation that practicing *Kuṇḍalinī sādhana* has deepened my experience and has reinvigorated my commitment to spiritual growth. I put on the editor's cap as an act of service, but this project has proved to be a wonderful opportunity for me to become more fully immersed in Nathaji's teachings, and to understand the distinctions between his teachings and those I had previously practiced and taught.

Swami Khecaranatha lives to serve, and is a fountain of love, inspiration, and guidance for all of his students. Throughout the editing process, he has been there in support whenever the enormity of the job overwhelmed me. I have grown in many ways from having done this work, and it has been an honor to do it. In that spirit, I gratefully offer my love and service back to my teacher.

—*Ellen Jefferds*

PREFACE

This book is a precious doorway into Swami Khecaranatha's lineage and teachings, and the spiritual power transmitted through them. Khecaranatha is one of the foremost disciples of Swami Rudrananda (Rudi), who was a truly remarkable man. As far back as 1959, Rudi sat at the feet of the great Nityananda of Ganeshpuri and received his spiritual power. Nityananda was a great saint who was well known and venerated throughout India. His most famous disciple was Swami Muktananda, who was one of the spiritual teachers of India who had the greatest following in the West.

Muktananda proclaimed to his disciples that Kashmiri Shaivism transmitted, in the most extensive and systematic form, the teachings that coincided most with his own experience and those of the *mahāsiddhas* of the past. This experience of the most elevated spiritual states, and the path that leads to them, he received through his assiduous practice—and, above all, the Grace of his guru Nityananda, a veritable embodiment in human form of Lord Śiva Himself.

In this book Khecaranatha chalks out his experience, which extends for over four decades, of the same path and the elevated states to which it leads. This he presents quite correctly as the "ancient practice of *Kuṇḍalinī sādhana*." Khecaranatha first tells us about his life, that of Rudi and Nityananda, and then guides us through the teachings of the Gurus of his lineage and his personal insights. This is not just a book about the path. It is a book to help those who are on the path. As deeply committed to those that follow after as he is profoundly grateful and devoted to the teachers before him, Khecaranatha declares his purpose and desire at the outset: "If this book proves to be of service to contemporary students of spirituality, it will have fulfilled its purpose." This is a book for such students.

Born an American, as was his teacher Rudi, Khecaranatha is living proof that the spiritual energy of *Kuṇḍalinī* does not make distinctions of birth. The transmission of spiritual energy from master to disciple crosses all the barriers of duality and difference. What matters is the "unbroken transmission of a living force."

This is the door that opens onto a vast world of inner experience and insight. Transforming as it elevates, it is the gentle yet immensely powerful Grace that fuels our inner growth and profoundly transforms our life. Khecaranatha, as a committed practitioner, talks to us directly, sharing decades of spiritual practice and careful observation. The books and manuscripts he has read and extensively researched are those that reflect his personal inner experience—his experience of "breath, *cakra*, flow, and presence."

The book is much more than a spiritual biography; it is a systematic guide to the concrete practice of *Kuṇḍalinī sādhana*. We learn how to develop the flow that awakens the living force of *Kuṇḍalinī* through the *suṣumna*, the vital axis of the subtle body. The configurations of the dynamic energies and inner forces govern and sustain the processes—physical, mental, and spiritual—which, working together, constitute both the substance and essence of the living being. Experiencing the power of this flow by regular practice, we are blessed with the gift of life. This is the Grace of Presence, namely, "the Goddess as pure light which emanates and creates from within the *suṣumna* and creates you."

Even as Khecaranatha guides us step by step through this practice, he helps us to understand ourselves. Paradoxically, we can only do this when we turn our attention away from ourselves and the fragmented dualities of life and focus instead on the fundamental Oneness that is the core of our Being and of all that exists. This change of perspective can only take place if we surrender to the One and abandon the ego with its countless claims, desires, frustrations, illusions, and false ambitions. These Khecaranatha carefully analyzes and teaches how to do that for ourselves.

The new perspective views life from the innermost center of our Being, not from the world outside and our concerns with it. When we turn our attention to our inner state, that is, the rhythmic vibration of Consciousness, we can ask ourselves the fundamental questions of life: "Where are we living?" and "What are we focusing on?" From this perspective we can find answers because our inner state "radiates out" and it's on that basis that we act, express ourselves, and experience the countless feelings that limit our lives.

While the innermost state is pure, unlimited Divine Consciousness, our outer state is in the grip of our ego—which is the mistaken notion of our identity as separate and different from others—and is continuously engaged in activity to maintain itself and fulfill its endless desires. Thus we are inevitably subject to frustration and conflict. This, then, is the source of our suffering. And there could be no way out if there were no inner state that enshrines our true identity and is a "living, conscious expression of Divine Presence, joy, and freedom." So we have a choice. Indeed, it is a choice we make every moment between unlimited, Divine Consciousness and the conditioned, frustrated ego of our mistaken identification with the body, mind, and personality, which is engaged in acquiring what it desires and avoiding what it fears.

When we choose the former, detachment, devotion to the One who is Lord of all, steadfast practice, and living in Grace develop within us day by day. We are transformed by the powerful forces of *śaktipāta*—the empowering Grace of Deity transmitted through the teacher that awakens *Kuṇḍalinī*. The same power of consciousness creates two possibilities. The first leads to a progressively more restricted experience of life, while the second, which is essentially the opposite, leads to expansion. We are all equally the same, unique Divine Consciousness, not countless, separate, self-confined egos. If we attend to Its Divine Presence within us, the power of Consciousness frees us from the grip of the ego. Then, we develop all the positive qualities such as compassion, devotion, discipline, surrender, joy, love, gratitude, and selfless service that contribute to our personal growth and fulfillment—and, by extension, the whole world.

These, in brief, are some of the most important teachings of this book. It is marvelous to see how Khecaranatha's experience coincides with the teachings of the Tantras in general and, most specifically, with the Kashmiri Trika school of Shaivism. Abhinavagupta, one of its greatest exponents, quotes a line that is so important that it appears in several Tantras of various Shaiva schools. It says, "this (liberating) knowledge has three sources that establish its validity: the teacher, the scripture and oneself." Abhinava comments that this is their order of importance. The teachings of the Master should be in harmony with the scriptures and these with one's personal insight.

Indeed, spiritual development is marked by the progressive expansion of consciousness, which unfolds the capacity for insight into the ultimate purport of the teachings, from the Master and the scriptures. As awareness grows, so do the spiritual qualities of devotion, selfless action, and inner joy eloquently extolled by Khecaranatha. As these qualities arise, the fundamental ignorance—which generates the mistaken sense of ego and duality, and the karma it creates—is gradually removed.

And so we discover, day by day, as Khecaranatha puts it, that "God dwells within you as yourself." Although this is the goal, the teacher is, as the Śiva Sutra declares, the means (*upaya*). As Abhinava says in his Tantraloka (The Light of the Tantras):

> *The people of this world, intent as they are on their own affairs, do not exert themselves to act for the benefit of others while he [the teacher] in whom all the impurity of phenomenal existence has been destroyed and is identified with God (Bhairava), by virtue of which he is full and perfect, has clearly only this (left) to do, namely, attend to the well-being of the world.*

> *Such is the extent of his graciousness that those, whose consciousness is pure by following that same course of development and who behold such a one, also became of his same nature.* (Chapter 2, verses 39 and 40)

Here, Abhinavagupta is alluding to a central feature of Khecaranatha's experience and teachings, namely, *śaktipāta*, the teacher's empowering Grace. *Śaktipāta* is imparted and received at first in the course of initiation. Indeed, that is initiation, which, maintained and renewed, is the beginning, the path, and the ultimate goal. Abhinava explains the nature of *śaktipāta* in great detail in chapter thirteen of his Tantraloka. There he tells us that there are three basic varieties of *śaktipāta*—intense, middling, and weak. Again, each one of these has these three degrees of intensity, making nine. He describes the first two degrees of the most intense form of *śaktipāta* as follows:

> *The intense-cum-intense descent of power spontaneously bestows liberation by the death (it brings about) of the body at that very moment (it occurs) or else (the soul may be liberated) at some other time (sooner or later) according to the degree (of Grace).*[1]

---

1 Thus, according to Jayaratha, the three varieties of Grace, each of which is three-fold, have three varieties according to whether the soul is freed of Mala, immediately, in a short or a long time. He says: In this way, in accord with its intensity and also because it has been said to be of three kinds, each one in this way has twenty-seven varieties.

Again, by the intense-middling (descent of power) all ignorance ceases (directly without the need of scriptures or teachers). That through which one knows by oneself[2] that one's own Self is (the cause of both) bondage and liberation is the great knowledge (born) of the divine insight (pratibhaa) (that comes by grace) independently (of the knowledge of the) scriptures or teachers.

The moon-like teacher whose (spiritual) darkness has been dispersed by the lunar rays of divine insight (pratibhaa), casting a glance[3] full of bliss (at his disciples), removes the darkness (of their ignorance) and the heat (of their suffering). (Tantraloka 13/129cd-133)

The disciples of Khecaranatha will immediately recognize that this is the way he received *śaktipāta* from his teacher and it is the way he imparts it, with, as he says, "eyes wide open." To see how this works according to the Shaiva and Shakta Tantras of the Trika, we need to examine briefly what they have to say about *śaktipāta*, initiation, and practice.

Śaktipāta removes the darkness of the restrictions that contract consciousness from its pervasive unlimited expanse down to a speck of light that is the essential consciousness in the core of our Being. Dualist Shaivites believe that these restrictions, which they call *mala* (literally meaning "impurity"), are an independent material substance that covers the consciousness of the individual soul. Accordingly, these Shaivites maintain that it can be removed by the appropriate action, as is chaff from rice by beating it, or a cataract from an eye by surgery. Initiation, they say, is the ritual action that removes the impurities. By the power of the appropriate mantras the teacher progressively leads his disciple's soul through the worlds of the cosmic order and their corresponding metaphysical principles up into Śiva, the

2 J: Independently of the other well-known instrumental cause, namely, the death of the body.

3 *drsham vispharya* lit. "expanding (his) vision" or "opening (his) eye"

highest principle. There, in Śiva's world, the teacher conjoins the disciple's soul with Śiva.

Kashmiri Shaivites accept that this procedure works but believe that it is slow and inefficient because it is not fueled directly by Śiva's Śakti. Moreover, the dualist perspective on which it is based is not correct. The best and most efficient way is to awaken *Kuṇḍalinī*, which from the non-dualist point of view, is equally both Śiva's Śakti and that of the individual soul. The former is called the "Upper or Raised *Kuṇḍalinī*," the latter the "Lower *Kuṇḍalinī*." Consciousness is the one reality, which we experience as Deity—who nourishes us and all Its creation with the power of Its empowering Grace. Through this force all things are created, sustained in their Being, and withdrawn back into Deity, who is Universal Consciousness.

Inherent in the freedom of Consciousness is the power to act and perceive. Consciousness makes of us perceivers and agents. It is the source of the awareness we have of ourselves and of the world that Consciousness manifests from within Itself. Consciousness passively illumines its manifestation within an unconfined expanse of power. Its own nature as the perceiver is derived from its own reflective awareness. As such, it operates as the power of knowledge. Operating as the power of action, consciousness is an agent, just as when it operates as the power of knowledge, it is a perceiver. Thus consciousness is Deity worshiped as Śiva and His power, Kuṇḍalinī Śakti, through which He generates all things— both individual perceivers and their objects. All this is manifested and known within Himself, like images in a mirror.

This, the pure freedom of consciousness, is the first aspect of *Kuṇḍalinī*, known as *Cit Kuṇḍalinī* (the *Kuṇḍalinī* of Consciousness). The second aspect is the *Kuṇḍalinī* of the Letters—*Varṇa Kuṇḍalinī*. The fifty letters of the Sanskrit alphabet represent aspects of the reflective awareness of Consciousness. These sounds stream in a timeless flow from A, the first letter of the alphabet, to H, the last.

A is the reflective awareness of *Anuttara*, that is, pure, absolute, *Bhairava* Consciousness. The following letters are the reflective awareness of the inner energies of Śiva and the outer metaphysical principles that emerge progressively to form the full expanse of manifestation at all levels. H is the reflective awareness of the plenitude of the outward flow of the stream of emission, which merges again into A. The cycle closes and perpetually replenishes itself, flowing round and within *Bindu*. Pronounced like the letter M, *Bindu*, which literally means "drop" or "point," is the dimensionless Center that serves as the axis around which the Wheel—*Cakra*—spins, and within which it is contained. Thus the fifty aspects of the flow of reflective awareness constitute the pure "I" Consciousness of AHAM. This is the dynamic energy of *Kuṇḍalinī* (Śakti), which generates, sustains, and withdraws the world of manifestation reflected in the pure mirror of Śiva's Divine Light.

We can experience this flow by paying attention, as Khecaranatha teaches, to the pulsing core of the Consciousness of our innermost Being. Here in the Center, free of all notions of difference, time, and space, we experience the supreme, perpetual flow of *Kuṇḍalinī*. Further out, as it were, in the physical and subtle body, the same flow manifests as that of the breath. Here we experience the flow of the *Kuṇḍalinī* of the Breath— *Prana Kuṇḍalinī*. The vital breath is the first transformation of consciousness. Withdrawing into Itself, Consciousness leaves behind an Emptiness into which it pours out as the vital breath. Travelling down the channel it opens up for itself, it generates and vitalizes the physical and subtle bodies. From this channel, called *suṣumṇa*, develop other channels from which others branch off until, like the veins of a leaf, they cover every part of the body.

Clearly, the central *suṣumṇa* is the most important. The vital force travels out from and back to its original source of pure Divine Consciousness. This flow stimulates the activity of the inner subtle body and the outer physical body. Thus the inner breathing of the descending and ascending flow of *Kuṇḍalinī* generates the outer breathing—that is, inhalation and exhalation.

We are not normally aware of this link. We do not normally experience the flow of *Kuṇḍalinī* without making an effort to do so, although it does sometimes happen spontaneously. Eloquently, and in great detail, Khecaranatha expounds the practice that arouses *Kuṇḍalinī*. From the point of view of practice at the corporeal level, we must wake up the sleeping, potential reflective awareness of this flow and accompany it with our attention, first up and then back down.

The ascending flow passes through a series of doors, levels, or configurations of energies—*cakras*—and pierces through the knots that block its ascent. At each stage the *Kuṇḍalinī* of the Breath vitalizes aspects of the physical, mental, emotive, and vital subtle bodies. As this takes place, lower, more contracted states are integrated into higher, more expanded ones, as *Kuṇḍalinī* moves through the energies of the elements—Earth, Water, Fire, Air, and Space—from which the body and the whole visible universe are made. One by one, the grosser lower elements are absorbed into the subtler, higher ones until we reach the mental sphere in the head and then out beyond it.

First exercising attention on the breath, then on the flow of the inner vital force of *Kuṇḍalinī*, aided initially by the imagination, we awaken our dormant awareness of this flow. In this way we "purify" it and it purifies us. We experience how the vital force leaves the body and reenters it, and so we learn, a little at a time, how to abandon the body to create a new, transformed body. Thus we benefit in two ways. First, we enhance our experience of ourselves and the world. Our physical, mental, and spiritual health all improve and are strengthened. Second, we learn how to leave the body. When, by our efforts, and above all, *śaktipāta*, we have perfected this practice of the art of dying, we recognise that we live because we do not die.

The Tantric traditions that focus on the worship of Goddesses such as Tripura, Kalī, and Kubjika, as well as those the Kashmiris considered to be the most secret and elevated, teach this higher form of initiation. It is called "Initiation by Piercing." Awakening the reflective awareness of this process by an intense descent of empowering grace—śaktipāta—the initiate experiences the Goddess Kuṇḍalinī rising through the cakras, piercing through them as She goes. In this way She burns up the impurities and ignorance that sully and condition consciousness through a process appropriately called "The Purification of the Elements." Ideally, this takes place just by the gracious look of the teacher, or by a touch, or just a thought.

The Anuttara Trika practices taught by Abhinavagupta accommodate both the slower method of ritual initiation and the more direct method of śaktipāta. The initiation by which the initiate ascends progressively through the metaphysical principles is done in its Trika form. This involves the visualization of Śiva's Trident projected along the axis of the body. The prongs extend out of the top of the head. On them, seated on Bhairavas, are the three Goddesses of the Trika Parā (the Supreme One), Parāparā (the Middle One), and Aparā (the Lower One). They are the three aspects of the one Goddess who embodies the triadic energy of Kuṇḍalinī. This is the common basic initiation. The direct awakening of Kuṇḍalinī in the Initiation by Piercing is the higher initiation and is considered to be the most excellent.

This form of higher initiation is the essence of the practice taught by Swami Khecaranatha. He has attained, through the transmission of his teachers and a lifetime of practice and personal experience, a deep understanding of Kashmiri Shaivism and Anuttara Trika. Thus, he summates, in his realization and teachings, what was considered by the Kashmiri Shaivites to be the most elevated teachings of all the Tantric schools—of which they were, without a doubt, the greatest exponents.

—Mark Dyczkowski, Ph.D., Varanasi, India

FROM THE AUTHOR, ABOUT HIS LINEAGE

A lineage is an unbroken transmission of a living spiritual force that is passed from heart to heart. It flows from one generation to the next—from a teacher to the student he wishes to initiate as a lineage carrier. Whether the initiation is an elaborate ceremony or simply the words of the teacher spoken to the heart of the person being initiated, it is the power of initiation that installs the seed of the living force in the recipient. Although this force manifests within a teacher, this living energy is greater than that which is carried within any person. A lineage carrier serves that force.

KUNDALINI SADHANA: THE PRACTICE OF THIS LINEAGE

Kuṇḍalinī sādhana, which some have dated back to 2000 B.C., has always been an inner practice carefully passed from teacher to student through oral and energetic transmission. While the emphasis on inner practice remained constant, a philosophical written tradition began to emerge in the seventh and eighth centuries.

These inspired writings and commentaries arose from the personal inner experiences of committed practitioners, and are based on their ardent study of the early Tantric practices. The significant philosophical expositions that arose from *Kuṇḍalinī* Yoga are Tantric Shaivism and Tantric Buddhism. Both are non-dualistic schools of thought. These practices and traditions blossomed from the hearts of early Tantric masters called *mahāsiddhas*. The term comes from *maha*, which means great, and *siddha*, which denotes a person who has attained perfection of inner awareness and energy. These *mahāsiddhas* were the preceptors of the earliest spiritual practices, and all of them were adepts in *Kuṇḍalinī* Yoga.

Throughout history there has been an underlying current of spiritual wisdom and energy that has manifested in various ways in many different times and places. Such a current preserves an unbroken connection with the Divine Source of living spiritual energy, and the *mahāsiddhas* are the preceptors of that Divine Energy in the Tantric tradition. A profound expression of that spiritual energy has most recently emerged through Bhagavan Nityananda and Swami Rudrananda (Rudi). They were modern-day *mahāsiddhas*, and the wellspring of my immediate lineage—extending the ancient practice of *Kuṇḍalinī sādhana* into the present.

As a lineage carrier in this tradition, I feel a deep gratitude to every teacher who has gone before me. They have passed down an enormous wealth of knowledge and have provided the practical tools to enable generations of seekers to gain their liberation. I have written this book to do my small part in perpetuating this vital teaching. If my words prove to be of service to contemporary students of spirituality, the book will have fulfilled its purpose.

SWAMI KHECARANATHA: A PERSONAL HISTORY

I was born in Illinois in 1951 but grew up in an international environment. When I was six, my family moved to Tierra del Fuego, Argentina. We lived there until I was twelve and then relocated to North Africa, in Tripoli, Libya. I didn't permanently return to the United States until 1970. Shortly thereafter, in October 1971, I met Swami Rudrananda.

In January 1972 I moved into Rudi's ashram in Indiana, and he recognized me as a teacher within this lineage later that year. After Rudi took *mahāsamādhi* in 1973, I continued to work with Swami Chetanananda, the spiritual leader of the ashram, and lived as a member of that community as it subsequently moved to Cambridge, Massachusetts, and finally to Portland, Oregon. Serving as the head teacher under Chetanananda, I was, through the years, instrumental in helping to develop the ashrams Rudi had started. In June 2001, I moved to Berkeley, California, to start TrikaShala, a spiritual practice under the auspices of Sacred Space Yoga Sanctuary. In addition to teaching, I currently serve as director of Rudramandir, a center for spirituality and healing, which is operated by Sacred Space.

Rudrananda and Chetanananda have given me wonderful opportunities to grow and to know God. They provided the spiritual nourishment, the guidance, the support, and the example. But my growth came from very hard work. The environment in which I grew up was as far away from Eastern spirituality as you can get. If I had followed the apparent direction of my life I would now probably be running a bait and donut shop somewhere down South.

What enabled me to pursue a different life? I would say two things: my extreme discomfort with the direction my life was heading, and Grace. Probably the two are inextricably related to each other. Perhaps it was Grace that gave me just enough insight into life to know that there must be more than *Monday Night Football* and *As the World Turns*.

Certainly it was Grace that led me to spiritual work. I was a declared atheist throughout my teenage years—so imagine my surprise when all of a sudden at age nineteen all I could think about was God! Soon afterward, through a series of not-so-coincidental events, I met Rudi. I had actually heard about him, without knowing his name, from a friend of mine who had seen him a year earlier. I came to realize that my friend was simply carrying the seed of my connection with Rudi to me.

My own meeting with Rudi demonstrates that it is possible, in one moment of life, for our experience and consciousness to be totally transformed. The unconditional love and powerful energy that radiated from Rudi penetrated deeply into me, cutting through what felt like lifetimes of confusion and pain. My heart exploded open—the first of many incredible gifts of Grace that I received from my teacher. Every moment since has been an expression of gratitude and devotion focused on growing. This focus is the best way I know to honor Rudi.

I only knew Rudi for about sixteen months in his physical form, but he gave me the most important understanding of my life: that spiritual freedom comes from a total dedication and effort to be free of our small self and to live in service to God. Rudi taught me through his life, through example, that unconditional surrender and service are imperative for anyone who wants to attain real spiritual growth. And for anyone who is granted the opportunity to teach, that becomes the fundamental platform for continued growth.

The unfolding of the spiritual process that was ignited when I was with Rudi has required tremendous work, but the commitment has been worth every minute and every ounce of energy it has taken. After more than forty years I can truly say that I am still witnessing Rudi's Grace unfolding in my life. I am even more committed in my work today than I was a year ago and know that a year from now I will find an even deeper devotion.

In July of 2002, I took formal vows of *saṃnyāsa* (sannyas) to reaffirm within myself what had been unfolding inside for many years—the desire to live in unconditional dedication to serving the Divine. I was initiated into the Saraswati Order by Ma Yoga Śakti, a swami who lives in New York City. I was given the name Swami Khecaranatha, which means "Moving in the fullness of the Divine Heart."

The literal translation of *saṃnyāsa* is "renunciation," but in the Tantric tradition this does not mean giving up the world and becoming a monk. Because the Tantric tradition recognizes that everything in creation is One, we don't seek to renounce the world but to experience the Unity of it. True renunciation is an inner state, and *saṃnyāsa* really means surrendering our small self or ego in order to know and serve that Unity.

Over the years I have attempted to live up to the vows of *saṃnyāsa*. That commitment was twofold—to find the Divine within myself, and to help others find that same Divinity in their lives. *Saṃnyāsa* means the total dedication of oneself to serving the Divine and the spiritual well-being of others. A swami, or *saṃnyāsin*, is unconditionally committed to serve, love, and support other people in their spiritual growth. To fulfill that undertaking, I continue to teach and to serve as the spiritual leader of a community of practitioners at TrikaShala.

SWAMI RUDRANANDA: HIS PRACTICE & TEACHINGS

Rudi called his practice "the work." He developed a powerful set of techniques, including a unique "open-eyes class" for the transmission of *śaktipāta* (shaktipat), an integral part of *Kuṇḍalinī sādhana*. Although he did not study scripture, Rudi's practice and teachings were a perfect expression of the most sacred of the Tantric Shaivite practices of ancient times.

Rudi was a complex man, but he lived in profound inner simplicity. He was extraordinarily powerful, yet gentle and full of Grace and love. Rudi was unconditionally focused on the dissolution of any limitation within himself as the means to allow God to emerge and reveal Himself. Rudi had been aware of his spiritual potential as a very young boy and spoke of continual inspirational visions and experiences that guided him on his path. His earliest teachers were Tibetan Buddhists, and he studied the teachings of Gurdjieff and Pak Subuh in his early twenties. However, Rudi's most powerful relationships were with the Hindu masters Sri Shankarcharya of Puri, Bhagavan Nityananda, and Swami Muktananda. It was the latter who recognized Rudi as a swami in 1966, and gave him the name Swami Rudrananda.

If I had to describe Rudi's spiritual teaching, I would say there are three elements central to his practice:

- opening the heart and cultivating a deep wish to grow
- working internally to establish a flow of energy through the psychic system
- living in a state of surrender

These three elements function as one dynamic. Rudi taught that they must be brought into our practice and into our lives every day. The discipline he required of himself and his students was the foundation of his teachings. He said that attaining liberation in this lifetime was our right, and that freedom was available to anyone who wanted it. Rudi emphasized that cultivating the wish would transform our experience and consciousness if we worked with depth over time. That depth is accomplished through opening our hearts, feeling the flow of spiritual energy within and with all of life, and surrendering to God.

In February of 1973, Swami Rudrananda departed from this world in a small plane crash in the Catskills. Remarkably, the other three passengers walked away with only minor injuries. Rudi's last words, dictated on the plane moments before it crashed, perfectly express the essence of his life and his teaching:

The last year of my life has prepared me for the deeper understanding that Divine Consciousness can come only through unconditional surrender. That state is reached by surrendering ourselves and the tensions that bind and restrict us, keeping us from expressing the power of creation that is our true essence. It is God flowing through us and showing us that we are nothing but Him. I want to live as an expression of that higher creative will, and from a deeper sense of surrender.

While Rudi had several teachers, it was his relationship with Bhagavan Nityananda that catapulted his growth into its most profound dimensions. Rudi said, "My first meeting with the renowned Indian guru, Bhagavan Nityananda, was of such a depth that it changed the course of my life." Although Rudi only met Nityananda a few times, it was the relationship that developed after the saint's passing that was the most important expression of their connection. Rudi described this profound relationship as existing on a spiritual level that was not limited by the absence of Nityananda's physical form.

BHAGAVAN NITYANANDA

Nityananda, whose name means "Bliss of the eternal," lived in southwestern India from around the turn of the twentieth century until 1961. Details of his early life are difficult to verify, but from the 1920s until his passing, he was surrounded by an ever-increasing number of disciples and devotees. By the late 1930s he was established in Ganeshpuri, a small village in the countryside near Mumbai, and an active ashram developed around him. In India today, Nityananda continues to be revered as a great saint.

Nityananda lived as the Divine expression of stillness, purity, and joy, and his teaching was profoundly simple. Like the ancient sages of many traditions, the essence of his teaching was that liberation occurs within every person when they merge their own individual consciousness into the Divine, and Nityananda clearly emphasized the awakening of the *Kuṇḍalinī* as the path to liberation. To realize the universal nature of one's own awareness, to be absorbed into the heart of God, is the goal of *sādhana* (spiritual practice).

The *Nityananda Sutras* outline the elements that are the essence of his experience, and therefore of his teaching:

- developing the subtle discrimination of seeing the One in the many
- cultivating detachment
- expressing devotion
- establishing an inner practice
- living in profound simplicity
- discovering unconditional joy
- living in Grace and in communion with the Divine

Nityananda often sat in a room in the ashram that was lit only by a few bare electric light bulbs, resting there quietly, with his eyes open. People came from considerable distances to see him because in India, the mere viewing (*darśana*) of a spiritual teacher is considered to be a profound blessing. The powerful forces of *śaktipāta* that continuously emitted from Nityananda permeated the environment around him. His presence attracted thousands of people, who wanted to receive his *darśana*. Each person who came in contact with this saint experienced the miracle of Pure Consciousness in human form. Bhagavan Nityananda was a holy person who was considered an *avadhūta*. Timeless and eternal, the *avadhūta* is a direct link to the Absolute, encompassing all the teachers who preceded him and all who follow.

"*Lightning, your presence from gound to sky.*
No one knows what becomes of me,
when you take me so quickly."

—*Rumi*

BOOK ONE

THE SECRET TEACHING

OPEN YOUR HEART,

FEEL THE FLOW,

SURRENDER EVERYTHING.

GO BACK TO PAGE ONE.

If we could simply open our hearts, feel the flow,
and surrender everything in this very moment,
we would find our freedom right now.

For most of us, however, we must do our spiritual
work with depth over time in order to find that freedom.
Boot Two will hep you to understand that journey.

BOOK TWO

Depth
Over Time

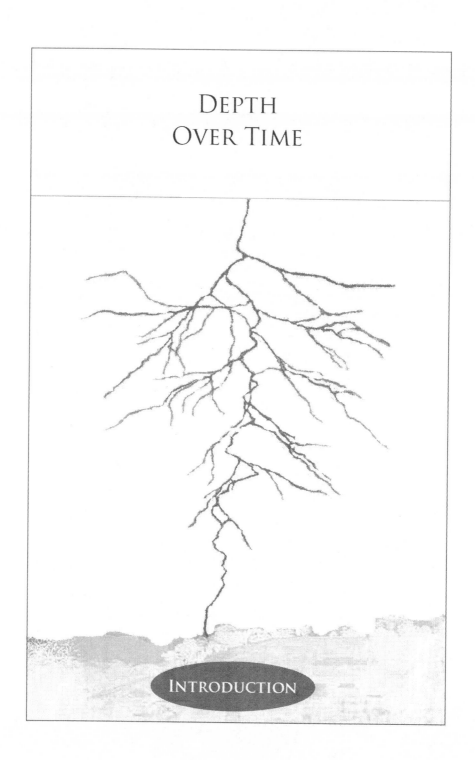

INTRODUCTION

INTRODUCTION

God dwells within you as yourself. The purpose of life is to discover that ultimate truth. We all have the opportunity to realize and attain liberation by raising our consciousness beyond the fundamental misunderstanding that we are separate from Divinity. It is God's Grace, combined with our deep wish to grow, that transforms our experience from duality to Unity. If we are very clear about what we want in our life and continually focus our life force toward that profound inner transformation, we can achieve it. Rudi succinctly expressed this when he said, "The equation for spirituality is depth over time." The title of this book was chosen to honor my teacher and to capture the essence of the journey of transformation and liberation available to each of us in this lifetime.

When lightning strikes and nears the ground, its energetic field magnetizes energy from the earth, drawing it up toward itself. The ascending force is not visible until it connects with the descending lightning. What we see is a pattern of light (called a "leader") that spreads and forks through the sky. As it nears the ground, the leader attracts an energy (a "streamer") that rises up from the earth. When the leader and streamer connect, a powerful electrical current begins flowing. The connection is complete and apparent.

This natural phenomenon beautifully mirrors the process of each person's spiritual transformation. As Grace descends, our individual wish ascends to meet it. Until the two meet, the current cannot flow. Is it the downward movement of Grace that lifts the ascending wish out of us? Or is it our wish rising, which pulls down Grace?

Whatever the answer, it is the joining, the union, that creates our experience. This contact completes a connection that allows the full force of the power of the Divine to strike us at the core of our being. The strike of Grace frees us from our limited understanding, allowing us to recognize that we are not separate, not different from our Divine Source. When this happens, our consciousness and experience of life is transformed.

There are many authentic practices that allow such a profound recognition to unfold. This book is a discussion of one of them, the ancient practice of *Kuṇḍalinī sādhana,* a Tantric practice that focuses on the merging of individual consciousness with Divine Consciousness. Tantric traditions use the terms Consciousness (Śiva) and Energy (Śakti) to describe the structure of life. Śiva's Supreme Consciousness is the foundation of all of existence, and the universe is the manifestation of Śakti's power to create. But underlying this discussion is the fundamental understanding that all of life is simply One Thing, beyond all duality.

This is not just philosophy or theory. It is our fortune that we are blessed with the possibility of realizing this truth. It is our birthright to experience this reality, and in order to live in that state of awareness, we must work to transform our consciousness, with depth, over time.

The power to create is the very foundation of every individuated life—of *your* individuated life. We are mirrors of our Divine Source. God's will and power have brought us into existence, and embedded in our psychic DNA is the God-given ability to be conscious, to use our will, and to act. It is important to understand that our will and power are not different from that of God, because this means we have been given the capacity to create the life we choose. It's a wonderful act of Grace that we not only have this power to create, but we also have the opportunity to liberate ourselves.

I once saw a documentary about the transformation of a caterpillar into a butterfly. It was visually quite beautiful, but what really intrigued me was the actual process of transformation. When it is ready to become a butterfly, the caterpillar crawls up into a tree and begins to wind a cocoon around itself. The first marvel is that the cocoon is not made of things gathered from the environment. The caterpillar extracts from within itself a thread, which it wraps around its body, creating the cocoon. From the outside, it looks hard and ugly—yet within the cocoon a miracle of nature begins to take place. A metamorphosis happens within this chrysalis as the caterpillar turns into what can only be described as "soup." It completely dissolves into a mush, and yet its essence is the same even though the form has changed. From that soup, the butterfly forms a new body with wings, and then eats its way out of the cocoon and flies off. The butterfly may only live for a short time, but it went through that incredible metamorphosis just for the opportunity to fly!

Another insight from this documentary is that according to the "butterflyologists" the caterpillar is conscious of what is about to happen. I don't know how many caterpillars were interviewed to discern this, and I don't really care, because the scientists' conclusion suits my point: Transformation is a conscious process that happens from within us. Life arises and subsides within the field of Consciousness Itself. Life is Consciousness pulsating into form, with form subsiding back into That. Consciousness itself never changes in this process. In the process of becoming, there is no diminishing of being, nor is there a diminishing of being as it subsides. The same vibrancy and consciousness is *always* there, giving us the power to choose to undergo a radical transformation even more miraculous than what happens to the caterpillar.

Life is always about the power of choice, the power to create, and the power to liberate. The choice is this: Do you want to live a life of joy or not? Understand that this is our fundamental choice in life. We have the power to create our lives, right down to every moment and every experience in it. *This is Your Life.* What is it about? We get to choose whether we live in the unconditional joy of freedom or in the pain and suffering of not knowing we are one with God.

In this book we are going to explore how we contact Divine Presence within us, and how this leads to living in God's Grace. Readers will hopefully come to understand the extraordinary transformation possible if we can truly open to Presence and allow it to permeate our lives. We can leave behind the person we have been and become a completely new person filled with God. Wouldn't that be amazing? So we will explore how we discover this potential in ourselves, and the work we must do to unfold and actuate it—both in terms of our conscious inner work and the conscious expression of that work in the world. We will also investigate what this transformation might feel like as we progress from living in the state of duality to the state of Unity. It is every human being's right to have that experience; it is the gift and the purpose of our life.

My advice is to choose the highest in life. Choose to live in the experience of freedom, pure joy, and unconditional love. Choose transformation and liberation. Choose to live in depth every day. Choose it over and over, again and again. Remember, the equation for spirituality is depth over time.

SECTION ONE

LIBERATION:
THE EXPERIENCE OF ONENESS

GOD IS ONE, WITHOUT A SECOND

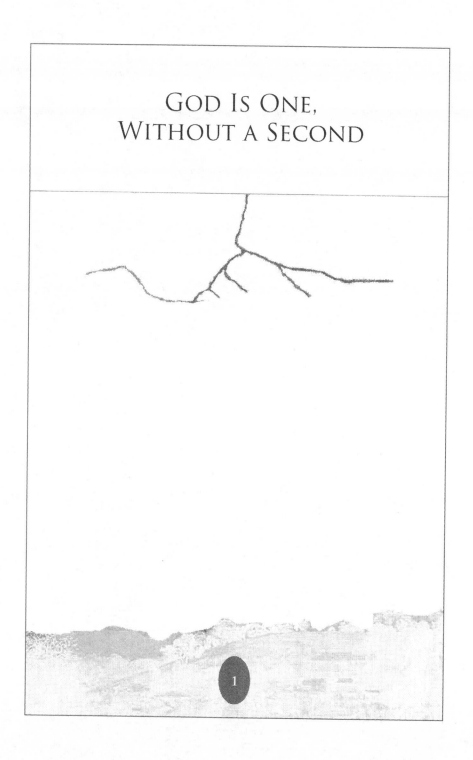

1

CHAPTER ONE

The Chandogya Upaniṣad was written three thousand years ago. Its entire exposition can be boiled down to this fundamental realization: "God is One, without a second." What an eloquent expression of the Divinity in all of life. Isn't it amazing that we hear the same thing from every great saint and every spiritual tradition? What is even more astonishing is that we do not believe it, that something doesn't explode in us saying, "That can be my experience." It is always shocking to me how day after day, we can deny the reality of our existence instead of reaching inside to understand it.

What is really meant by the expression "God is One"? This is not a feel-good greeting card statement or a platitude like "It's a Small World After All." Rather, it is the expression of a profound, literal understanding—and a direct experience available to every human being—that all of creation is simply One Thing. Attaining this realization requires a lifetime of transformation. It is a transformation that will fundamentally shatter every limited perception we have of life, because the experience of Oneness is so radically different from how we normally perceive and live in the world.

What is this One Thing? We can call it "God"—and generally that is how it will be referred to in this book—or we can use other terms such as Divinity or Pure Consciousness. When we speak of God, we are referring to that Supreme Consciousness from which all of life arises. We can also talk about the way we experience God, as Divine Love or Divine Presence. One of these terms will perhaps resonate better for each reader, but the words themselves are not what are most important.

TRANSCENDING DUALITY

In any tradition, the most important understanding is that the entire process of spiritual growth is one of transcending duality. It is transcending the misunderstanding that we are separate from our own Source. There is an analogy that is very simple, yet serves as a profound illustration of this fundamental point. We can think of our individual existence as being like a drop of water in the ocean. In reality, we are not different or separate from the ocean but an individuated expression of that whole. Identifying ourselves as being a unique drop of water, we believe we are distinct from the larger body of water and perceive duality where none actually exists. It is through our spiritual work that we gain the direct realization that we, as individuals, are not separate from the whole. We are simply a living expression of the Divine.

The vital force that creates and sustains the universe lives within us, and is buried in us. Even if we do not consciously connect to it, it is still there. In the Tantric tradition, this force is called *Kuṇḍalinī*, the energy within the psychic body, which lies dormant in the base of the spine. Because the power of the universe is in us, we can learn how to find and connect to it. When we begin to activate this power, it dislodges any interior obstacles that block the *Kuṇḍalinī* energy from rising. This is the process that eventually reunites us with our Divine Source.

Tantric traditions describe the structure of life in terms of there being a silent ocean of infinite Consciousness (Śiva) and a creative, active force (Śakti, Goddess, or Kuṇḍalinī). Kuṇḍalinī, by Her very power to manifest everything in creation, also has the capacity to hide Her silent Source. Our experience as human beings is that we get absorbed in this manifestation, in the act of living, and forget that within the very fabric of creation there is only the Oneness of God.

Oneness can be experienced as the nature of who we are, and each of us has some resonance with the statement "God dwells within me as myself." However, every preconceived idea we have of this reality is incorrect—because it is only when we are immersed in the experience that we come to know the truth of it. This isn't theory. It isn't a novel someone wrote. It is the ultimate truth, and the purpose of our life is to discover that both Śiva and Śakti are present within us as our Self.

Śiva is Supreme Consciousness and the foundation of all of existence. He knows who He is. He also knows what He wants to create and has the power to do so. From within the stillness of Consciousness, a pulsation arises, which turns into creation. This is described as dynamic stillness—"dynamic" referring to energy and "stillness" to Pure Consciousness.

Traditionally, there has been endless discussion about who is more powerful, who came first, Śiva or Śakti? The Shaktas say that Śiva is just inert consciousness, and the Shaivites say that without awareness Śakti has no function. So it's a wonderful, circular debate that no one can win.

In reality, eternal Consciousness and the power to create are not separate. Everything one can see through the Hubble telescope is the Goddess expressing Herself, manifesting through Her power to create. If the Goddess dwells within us as ourselves, then all of Her power exists within us, and this is the power we use every day to create our life. So the question immediately arises, "If I have this power, what am I creating with it?" This brings us to the reason we engage in a spiritual practice, the reason we start to focus and clarify our intention—so that we can tap into that God-given power within, to create the very life we say we want.

SHIFTING OUR ATTENTION

We open the door into inner stillness and Divine Presence by finding a place of profound simplicity within ourselves. This has nothing to do with how complex our life is. All of the diversity, complexity, and multiplicity in the entire universe are an expression of One Thing, one single pulsation of the Divine. We seek to transcend our own duality and sense of separation from our Source, but we do this through the expressed diversity in our lives, not by retreating into a cave. This experience is available to each of us in what Bhagavan Nityananda called the "heart-space" or the "sky of the heart." Getting in touch with and living from that heart-space is the single purpose of our life.

We can also talk about spiritual growth or transformation of consciousness in terms of the dissolution of the ego. The ego creates its own reality in itself and in the world. We project our misunderstanding from our ego, from the part of ourselves that believes it is separate from its own Source. So how can we do anything but create duality in our perception of the world, which we see as being "out there"? We not only project *onto* something we believe is outside of ourselves—so instantly there is the perception of "two"—but we project *from* a place of duality within us, from a place of profound misunderstanding.

The ego is not our personality but rather the aspect of us that adamantly believes we are separate from our Source. The issue is what we engage—the part of us that identifies itself as being separate, or the part that knows it is One with God. Spiritual practices are called such because they involve training our awareness and attention. We can also view this as retraining, because most of us have grown up projecting into the world. When we project that vital force outwardly it creates duality, but when we learn to direct it inward, it brings us to the unity of life. The purpose of spiritual practice is to reorient ourselves so that we function from a place of deep stillness within, a place that can transcend the grip of the ego.

To understand and experience Unity, we must bring our energy inside and not get distracted by superficial longings. Over and over again, we forget our focus and then wonder why we have not found what we are seeking. Ask to know God. Decide that this is what you want in your life. That profound experience and awareness is available to all of us, if we want it more than anything else. Unless spiritual freedom is the single focus of our lives, we probably won't attain it.

MOVING BEYOND OUR RESISTANCE

Everything that gives us instant gratification comes with a price, and that price is suffering. Until we find a place of unconditional joy and fulfillment within, we will continue to find only temporary happiness. We hold on to things, and we hold on to the concept that some situation in our lives is not right. We keep waiting for circumstances to be perfect. Continually looking for the same thing, from the same place in ourselves, we repeat deeply ingrained patterns of behavior. Even if we regularly have the experience of making contact with a deeply profound, quiet, fulfilled place inside, all too often we still gravitate back to looking for external satisfaction.

When we forget to focus within, we must keep coming back inside, again and again. We forget, and then we start rejecting ourselves, which immediately reinforces our perceived separateness. Although it's true that we repeatedly misunderstand our experience, we do not need to berate ourselves about it—nor should we go to the opposite extreme and anesthetize ourselves with drugs, power, money, or sex. We all know individuals who live in extraordinary drama, pain, tension, and insanity on a daily basis. We have to make the conscious decision to focus on the part of us that remembers that we are God. If we slip from that resolution, we reach inside and start again.

Abhinavagupta was a mystic and philosopher who lived in the tenth to eleventh centuries and is regarded as one of the great saints of Tantric Shaivism. He said that a person with earnest intent could sit down and find realization in four forty-minute sessions. The only requirement was to have enough depth of longing. Today, some teachers even say that all you have to do is open your heart and know reality, without engaging in any spiritual practice. Unfortunately, for almost all seekers, this is not their experience. Through the power of attention, we must choose our realization over and over again until it actually happens. The real problem is getting past the moments we do not choose it.

That is why I pose the question: Doesn't our realization ultimately depend on how much we want it, right here, right now? It is part of the extraordinary paradox of Unity, and of our own experience, that if we could sit right now and reach into the depth of our heart, we would have that realization in a flash. Yet this happens for so few of us. The rest of us have to work at it and grind it out. Divine Presence, that radiating, pulsating pure love, is giving birth to us moment by moment eternally, beyond time and space. It is always present in our lives. There is never a second in which God's Presence and love are not available to us. Do not think of realization as something that happens "later." It is something we must continually focus on, and our one-pointed devotion to finding that liberation is what will bear fruit over time.

THE POWER OF LONGING

Our longing is what connects us to a palpable experience of God. It arises from our awareness and connects us to the Divine Consciousness that is expressing Itself as us. The Sufi poet Kabir said that in the search for God, it is the intensity of the longing that does all the work. He then added, "Look at me and you will see a slave to that intensity." It is this passionate desire to know

God that brings us to the place of practice every day, and it is what fuels the deepening of our practice over time. We cultivate that longing by breathing into it, expanding it, and allowing it to grow.

Some part of us remembers God and desires to be reunited with that Supreme Consciousness. We wish to tune in more deeply to the Divinity already present within us. Longing creates the fire that burns up all the obstacles to our spiritual growth. God is always singing, and we are the song. We are the notes. Having a sense of profound longing means we are pregnant with our wish to grow. The intensity of the desire is powerfully transformative because it brings us to a place in ourselves that wants something more than the mundane, surface experience of day-to-day living. Everyone has the wish to grow, because this longing is God wanting to know Himself again.

What do we do if we don't feel the deeper longing? Find it. If we only have a faint impulse, then the work is to get inside, tune in to it, and ask and ask for the longing to intensify. Rudi often said, "Within a human being, the wish is the most powerful force in the universe." We suffer because we choose less, and then hate ourselves for having made that choice.

Longing is a fire that will transform us, so we should celebrate it. When released within, the energy of that fire does all the work. We hear it so many times and we don't believe it. We don't believe God dwells in us as ourselves and is ceaselessly trying to show us our Divinity. How interesting! We have the opportunity to transform our lives, and it is vital to bring extraordinary joy to our spiritual work, not the anguish of separation. The joy naturally arises from the knowledge that we are going to find God in ourselves. Think of the powerful difference of vibration this orientation immediately creates. Anguish is very dense and hard, and joy is simply full of light.

The Sufis also say that spiritual growth is not the journey to God, but the journey in God. This is a profound expression of simply being immersed in and being expressed from that Source. Shouldn't we celebrate this? We want to discover a deeper place of consciousness within ourselves, one that is always tuned in to God. Otherwise we will spend a lifetime lamenting the fact that we are not experiencing Divinity. When we feel longing, it is an expression of Divine Love and Grace trying to help us remember our own Source. We either consciously choose to respond to that offer or unconsciously choose to ignore it. So often we don't listen to what is trying to unfold within us. The subject line of the email says "Higher Love." We get the email and delete it, marked as spam. Why not read it instead? God might have something important to tell us!

GOD DWELLS WITHIN

Deep within each of us is the knowledge that the Divine is the Source of our lives. Our spiritual work is to develop and refine our tuning mechanism so that we can resonate on the same frequency as the subtle Divinity that is expressing all life, to palpably connect with it. The psychic body and the *cakra* (chakra) system function as this mechanism, and there are specific techniques we can use to unfold its potential. Everything we talk about and all the practices we do relate to one single thing—that what we seek is the experience of God loving us. We need to explore this within our hearts and try to understand why we don't always experience God's love, even though it is always being offered.

Think of the incredible richness and fulfillment we would experience every moment in our lives if we were tuned in to the effulgent expression of limitless Spirit that is available to us. However, it is important to avoid thinking that this experience is "out there," either outside us or in the future. The place to start is right here, right now. We must focus on how full our lives already are, not on how full our lives could be. This means tuning in to a different dimension of life—the part of us that remembers its Source, not the part that has forgotten. Otherwise, we will spend our energy reinforcing and reinvesting in some limited vision of what we think of as life. When we do that, it becomes our reality and we are resonating with a slower, denser vibration. In a sense, a higher vibration is like a high-pitched frequency that requires us to develop a very finely calibrated inner radio receiver.

Tuning in to Divine Love means we are filled with it, and we function within the dimension of it. This does not mean that life is suddenly filled with bliss and love. Outward circumstances might not change at all, but our perception of them is transformed. Even though we continue to experience difficulties and pain, we are grounded in a place within us that is not affected by the surface dimensions of life.

A conscious person has the ability to function on at least two dimensions at once, if not on multiple dimensions. Most people get completely caught up in the dynamics of their life as they know it, and because they can't see these higher dimensions, they don't seek them.

We have to redirect the energy we normally expend outward in reaction to external circumstances. By reorienting our attention inward and living from our center, we change from the inside out. We can waste time talking to ourselves all day about how miserable we are, complaining about our life, instead of finding a different resonance. Meditation is tuning in to our own Source. This is what allows a lightness and a deeper understanding to begin to filter up through all the denser levels within us, so that these qualities can become manifest in our awareness.

THE DEPTH OF TRANSFORMATION

The goal of spiritual work is to live in a permanent state of Divine Presence, and so we must become a new person, more deeply filled with God, if we want that realization. Every one of us has to ask, "Has my life worked? Have I filled myself with Divine Presence?" The answer can fall within a spectrum from "Yes, maybe, I don't know, I'll know when it happens" to "Absolutely not, I live in misery." Of course, what happens as soon as we start asking ourselves these questions is that a whole litany of reasons, excuses, and causes pop up to explain why we haven't yet found that Presence. We get tense, and we accept all these reasons as valid explanations for why we haven't become a new person, why we have not allowed God to fill us.

None of the reasons we use to explain our separation are valid. They are real, but not valid. However, where we start our spiritual practice is not important. To be made new is to leave every pattern, contraction, and rationale behind, and to open into a new place within.

Only in a state of internal spaciousness do we have the capacity to receive and absorb something higher. We want to discover how to let go of all the things that keep us separate, how to empty ourselves of everything that has filled us. It is really amazing to look at how we invest our life force. We continually fixate on the very things that keep us from penetrating the depth in ourselves. Why do we do this? Why have we let our tensions taint interactions with the people we say we love? How do we change this pattern of surface thinking and reach into a place within that can reveal extraordinary freedom and profound joy? If we haven't found Divine Presence where we have been looking, we need to look somewhere else. The Sufi poet Rumi wrote, "You've been stony for too many years. Try something different. Surrender."

In order to become a new, realized person, the ego must be transcended. We must be free of the part of us that holds on and loves to suffer. The ego absolutely, fundamentally believes it is separate from God. Because it seeks to protect its separate existence, the commitment we have to make is to tune in to a different frequency and resonance, the Divine Love and stillness within. We need not focus on killing the ego. It is more accurate to say that the ego will die or fall away as Divinity emerges in our lives. We are simply letting God show Himself. When you peel away all the excuses, the reason we continue suffering is that we choose to do so. We must make the choice to enter into another dimension entirely — one that is unconditionally free.

We are completely loved by our own Source at all moments — but when we can't get in touch with that, we look for love everywhere else. And although we will find love in other places, it will not sustain us if we don't have it in ourselves. We have to love the Divinity within. Once we are established in that place, the outer love in our lives will have much more joy and much more meaning. We live in a state of duality in which we think there is "inner life" and there is "that world out there." But this conception is fundamentally unreal. Our outer life is an expression of our inner self. Even the most challenging people in our lives are an expression of some part of us that we need to learn to love. How we relate to them is dependent on where we live within ourselves. The world is just a reflection of that inner place.

Perhaps the miracle of Grace is that in spite of all of our efforts to reject it, Divine Love is there, always available to us. To allow Divine Presence to be revealed, we must open to receive it. This requires that we are prepared to sacrifice our unwillingness to open, to let go of our attachment to suffering. Each of us has an extraordinary opportunity to find a fulfillment beyond our imagination. At any moment we can have a profound experience that can transform us forever. Kabir once said that he saw the Secret One for fifteen seconds, and that was enough to make him a servant for life. My corollary to that is, "I will become a servant for life to see God for fifteen seconds."

Living a spiritual life means choosing a higher vibration, resonance, and awareness. We perpetually want to think that at some point we will stop suffering, because external life will change and suddenly life will be utopian. We have believed that, lifetime after lifetime! The reality is that the dynamics of our life may not fundamentally change, but we can transform our experience of life. The process of creating this shift in awareness is achieved through our inner practice and by having a relationship with a teacher, who serves as our connection to a living spiritual force. It takes extraordinary courage to admit to ourselves that we need the love a teacher can offer, and to have the vulnerability to say, "I need help. I need to be nourished." More than anything, the willingness to receive from a teacher and from God is what we need to bring to our wish to grow.

The reason it is possible to become a new person filled with Divine Presence is that when we make contact with it, Presence itself obliterates everything we are holding on to, everything we mistakenly think of as ourselves. We discover we can let go of all the things that keep us separate from God. The essence of spiritual work is the dissolution of our individual identity, which is caught up in how we have been defining ourselves. This limited self thinks it is separate from its own Source, and for that reason it is hard to talk about or describe Divine Presence. If I say that Divine Presence is "a state of unbounded Consciousness," how is that understood by someone who can only experience limitation and separation? Perhaps it is easier to relate to a description such as, "We can experience Presence as a complete state of profound joy." The latter statement is not as direct a challenge to the ego's perspective.

Trust, or surrender, is the foundation required to build a life established in Divine Presence. If we are honest with ourselves, every time we get tense and contract, every time we suffer, it is because we do not trust the God within us. Trust does not mean giving up or giving in. When we trust and surrender, we are saying, "Hallelujah, let my life express itself in its full Divinity." The challenge is to become a new person who lives from a different place—one in tune with God's heart. There is a Divine force at the core of life that expresses Itself as us, and as everything around us. The only way to know this is to experience it for ourselves, and so we must surrender, trust, and let God emerge and unfold from within us. Many people are called to spiritual work, but very few choose it.

Freedom in This Lifetime

Chapter Two

Jīvanmukti is a beautiful term in Sanskrit that means "freedom in this lifetime." Let us understand, celebrate, and explore how this state can be realized in our own lives. If someone said to you, "Unconditional freedom is the Divine right of every individual; to live in that state is to live in Divine Presence," how would you react? If we want freedom, the thing we must feel is, "That is my right. I believe that." Unfortunately, for most of us, this is not something we truly believe is our right—and therefore we do not seek it. We are not prepared to become a professional at spiritual work in order to achieve that state.

Realization can be described as the complete immersion into Unity, a state in which the only experience is one of unconditional joy and love. These words hint at the nature of true freedom, but words cannot express the reality of living in God's Presence. Because the reality is like nothing we can express, Rudi once said that so much of the challenge to our realization is our inability to imagine it. Try to imagine extraordinarily profound joy, and then multiply your vision one thousand times and you will not even come close. Yet somehow, there is some part of us that knows, and seeks to make that dimension of life a living reality.

It is important to understand that although awakening can happen at any moment, it takes a lifetime to actualize our enlightenment—for that transformation of consciousness to permeate every layer of our lives.

Even when we have a profound experience of our own Divinity, there is still the need, every day, to make the conscious choice to reinvest and internalize that awareness back into ourselves. This is how we transform our experience into a state we always live in and function from. It's due to Grace that we have this experience, and then we have to integrate that new awareness and allow it to express itself in our life. We seek to be free of the limitations of our body, mind, and emotions, but we want this to be a living reality, not something we attain after death. In fact, if we don't attain freedom while we are alive, we won't gain it after we have died.

FINDING FREEDOM WITHIN

We cannot find freedom in the world. We have to find liberation in ourselves, and then express our freedom in the world. It does not work the other way around. Where shall we experience living in Divine Presence except within ourselves? We first go inside and discover that freedom, and then understand how it is expressed through our outward life. Living in freedom means flowing with every moment—accepting everything we encounter and letting go of the need to change anything. In order to live in Divine Presence, we must choose to not live in our own tensions and limited self. Therefore, if we are serious about finding freedom, we must also develop the ability to change our inner reality.

One of the significant tenets of *Kuṇḍalinī sādhana*, as part of the Tantric tradition, is that while freedom happens from within us, there is nothing in the outer world that needs to be rejected in order to find our realization. Freedom is the rejection of nothing, and the inclusion of everything. Because there is no duality, there is no ultimate difference between our inner and our outer experience—and perhaps, coming to that understanding is the true meaning of freedom.

When we look at what keeps us from our freedom, we find that the ego seems to be as powerful as Divinity. It has a firm grip on us. The ego thinks it is real and the center of the universe. Its belief in its separate status is an illusion that dominates our awareness to such a degree that if we wish to transform ourselves, we must consciously choose to do so. We must proactively choose freedom and Grace, because we are otherwise allowing our limitation, tension, and ego to reinforce the hold they have over us.

Einstein said, "You can never solve a problem on the level on which it was created." The problem of the ego is its misunderstanding. We can't chip away at our ego from the outside without first dissolving it from the inside. So often we are unwilling and unable to deeply open our hearts and feel love pour into us—and then we never find a different place in ourselves from which to combat the boundaries and the prison of the ego. God's love is the only thing that can penetrate this density. We must allow the Divine Force within us to emerge. When that happens, the ego can be dissolved.

If we try to change the ego from the outside, we will not be able to do it. Even if we are successful at changing some of our patterns or our personality, we are just modifying something superficial, like the clothes we wear. Although this is where most people want to focus, it really has nothing to do with the ego. We can say, "I will change, I can behave differently." We can—but the dissolution of the ego, the immersion into our own Divine Self, has nothing to do with personality. In the deepest sense, it has nothing to do with our day-to-day behavior. It has to do with the complete dissolution of the misunderstanding that we are separate from God, and more importantly, with the actual experience of our unity with that Divine Presence.

Once this transformation begins to happen, the Self emerges from within us, and the core attachment the ego uses to bind us begins to dissolve. The ego falls away. This process of dissolution is inherently painful, especially if we only focus on it from the outside, from the point of view of what is dropping away. But if we focus on what is emerging from within we are joyous about the process. As we start to experience the profound fulfillment and infinite space within us, we are motivated to strengthen our commitment to growth. We are trading up—trading in our ego for a Divine Life.

Transcending the ego does not mean that we douse it with kerosene and throw a match on it. Rather, this is a process of expanding beyond the limited egoic perspective. Our work is to recognize that although this perspective is part of the matrix of what we experience ourselves to be, it is not all that we are.

In our attempt to expand beyond the boundaries of the ego, we must learn to consciously discriminate between that which is going to attune us to the highest place within ourselves and that which doesn't serve us. When making choices about our lives, we don't surrender the infinite possibility; we surrender our fear.

Where do we find fear? What does it really look like? It is energy. It has no form and yet we translate it primarily into form. What we actually fear is giving up our attachment to form; giving up our attachment to the limitations we are used to and that define who we think we are.

THE CHALLENGE OF FINDING GOD

The profound superficiality we humans are willing to accept in ourselves denies us the depth that is available within. Ironically, it is the very joy and happiness of everyday life that can cause us to get complacent about our limited experience. That is why God provided a few challenges in our lives—to force us to look for a deeper reality. Regardless of what we experience on the surface of daily life, God dwells within us as ourselves, and what is available to us is unbounded and unlimited. It is always our choice to remain on the superficial level of life or to engage in the process of transformation. And while the first option is in some ways easier, the reward of doing the work needed to truly live in freedom is worth all the effort.

If we do not experience profound fulfillment, then there is some part of us that is still not free. The purpose of our lives is to live in unbounded joy and freedom. The trick God has played on us is that He gave us freedom and then put a container of lead around us, which we have to break our way out of in order to have that experience. Tantric philosophy says that Śiva and Śakti decided to get together and apparently lose themselves in the world—to intentionally forget themselves so that they can experience the joy of remembrance, the joy of finding themselves again.

The paradox of Divine life is that both freedom and binding exist within us. What part of us gets expressed is our choice. God invested a power in us to create whatever life we want, and this includes the possibility that we cannot remember our Source. We get caught up in one level of manifestation, thinking it is the only reality. Life is infinite. Creation dances on the field of Consciousness, taking the form of everything in the universe, including our individuated lives. Form is Consciousness pulsating into manifestation. That is how we get here and become part of the play and the beauty of God's creation. How wonderful.

FINDING INNER PEACE IN A TROUBLED WORLD

I am not particularly a believer in the assertion that we will experience world peace, but I am a believer in inner peace, because we each have the ability to control this dimension of life. We are able to control where we live in ourselves and whether or not we are happy. We can certainly be conscious of the world in general, but we must keep our focus on our inner world, on saving ourselves, and unfolding freedom from within.

One of the real challenges for people is the illusion that humanity should be perfect. We read in the news about terrible things that go on in the world, and we believe they should not happen. But such things do take place, again and again. This doesn't mean they're right, but it means they do, in fact, happen. As with any experience, we have a choice about how we react to what arises in our lives. Allowing the news to affect our state is a choice *we're* making, because we think, "Something occurred that shouldn't have happened."

Throughout recorded history, very unfortunate events have continually taken place. Why? Rudi gave the perfect answer when he said, "The reason the world is screwed up is that nobody opens their heart." That's the underlying reality—and therefore what we each have to be responsible for is opening our own hearts as big as we can to the people around us. And while we do have compassion when things happen to those who aren't part of our life, we can't really allow that to affect our state.

When we permit world events to deeply affect us, we have consented to being closed down. Justifying this reaction becomes another excuse to live in our humanity instead of transforming our consciousness and living in the Divinity available within us. We can get so caught up in the evil that's happening in the world that we completely lose contact with ourselves. We lose contact with the profound opportunity to grow beyond the limitations of inner constriction. It takes a lot of discipline and consciousness to really stay in touch with our center and not get lost when we experience something we perceive to be negative.

Everyone has karma in this life, and the "bad" things that happen to people reflect the fact that their karma has created this situation for them. This does not mean they're bad people, but it probably means they are now reaping the results of their past actions. We must understand that every person is an individuated expression of one Divine whole, and the dynamics within a person's journey back to their own Source involve a few bumps in the road. And most of those bumps were attracted from within themselves, often not even in this lifetime. Just by looking at external circumstances, we cannot know the value of what someone else is experiencing.

WE BUILD OUR OWN INTERNAL PRISONS

I once read an article about an interview with a Tibetan monk who had been imprisoned and tortured for twenty years by the Chinese. When asked if he hated his captors for taking away his freedom, and whether he'd lived in fear all those years, the monk's response was simply incredible. He said his only fear was that he would close his heart and thereby lose his freedom. Here was a simple person, not some great saint—and yet he was able to find in himself the capacity to let go of the harsh conditions that life presented, recognizing that only he himself could take away his true freedom. I guess you could say he *was* a saint.

Most of the time, we build our own prisons. We create walls of tension around our hearts because we're continually, forcibly trying to change what God has given. It is not ultimately relevant whether a situation is right or wrong. Was it right for the Chinese to have imprisoned this monk for twenty years? Not relevant, in terms of what was going on for him as an internal process. We can only imagine the work, the deep surrendering that a person in that kind of circumstance must have gone through to enable him to come out of this experience without any hatred, without any need for revenge—without anything except the thought "I held on to my freedom, I kept my heart open." Taking into account the amazing lesson this monk learned from his suffering, can any of us absolutely say that what happened to him should not have happened?

We must raise our perspective—have the jet airplane view as we're flying through life. The things we want to build into big dramas are not in themselves what they seem, and we have to be careful not to let our emotional state be hooked into those situations. It doesn't mean we lack compassion or don't care. The best thing we can do for people in difficult situations is send them love and joy, instead of imposing our opinions on them. It might also serve us to remember that in their deepest selves, the perpetrators are in as much pain as those on the receiving end of their actions. We need to have compassion for those people too. And that's harder in our mind, but not harder in our heart. If we understand from a higher perspective, it's just as easy to have love and compassion for the people who have done something that seems abominable as it is to feel for their victims. We really only hear about 1 percent of what happens on a daily basis. And what goes on outside of this country is infinitely worse. We simply cannot relate to it in its own dimension or we will go crazy. We will shut down.

So let's simply focus on the extraordinary things that are happening on this planet. Good or bad, we only applaud or dislike what happens from our limited perspective. When we find ourselves caught in our mind or our emotions about some situation, we have an extraordinary opportunity to open our heart and say, "No, I will not live in my mind, in these thoughts. I will not live in this place that's closing." We choose instead to focus on our own purpose in life, to establish ourselves in God's joy at every moment. What an amazing transformation of our consciousness to even have the awareness to attempt that shift, instead of getting pulled out of ourselves in some drama we can do nothing about, and will not change.

We should take responsibility for transforming our own behavior if we want to change the world. We must keep our hearts open and treat the people in our immediate sphere with as deep a love and respect as we can. Much as we'd like to be responsible for others—even those closest to us—they are not our responsibility. And unfortunately, trying to help our friends and loved ones usually takes the form of trying to control them! However much we might wish to beat our friends and family into being our idealized version of them, we should avoid this temptation.

Although we hope for the best for those dear to us, and wish for world peace, the reality is that our desires may not be fulfilled. We may feel that this is unfortunate, but it does not have to affect our inner state. And perhaps if a lot more people attempted to transform themselves, there would be more chance of world peace. Let's really be responsible for what we can be responsible for. And perhaps as the number of people we can love grows, then we can have some impact.

OPENING TO THE VERTICAL DIMENSION

If we do not open to the vast possibility of freedom within us, we remain on a level where we often experience suffering. And yet we have the opportunity to live from a very different place, where we can be full of joy, regardless of our external circumstances. The apparent contradiction in the fact that life can be full of both suffering and joy is only resolved by gaining the ability to operate on more than one dimension at the same time, and this is accomplished through the power of our own attention. My own experience is that we choose in every moment where to place our attention, and those moments define our lives. If we are not consciously growing a Divine Life, then we are unconsciously allowing it to remain limited.

We all operate on many dimensions at the same time. We have our physical body, our mental and emotional body, our psychic body, plus our eternal, Divine body—and there are innumerable other dimensions in between these as well. Although we function within all these dimensions, a spiritual person tries to connect to the highest within, without rejecting, abandoning, or losing contact with the rest. From the top, we can always see all the way down to the bottom, but from the bottom we can't see the top. So it is only when we are aware of the highest that we can make the conscious choice of what dimension to live in.

This is not a discussion about the relative roles we play in our lives. Roles are the horizontal unfoldment of those different dimensions within us. We're human, so we have to pay our rent and have a profession, but this is only the surface activity we perform while living on earth. We grow by consuming each level of horizontal life, pulling its energy inside us so that the force can move us up to another level of horizontal life, which we again internalize. The next chapter will offer a detailed discussion of what it means to internalize energy and put it into the vertical flow. The relevant point, however, is that attaining freedom is ultimately the complete transcendence of any horizontal life. From the highest perspective, everything is vertical.

COMMITMENT AND DISCIPLINE

There is a profound depth of consciousness at our Source. It is always available to us if we tune in to it. If we do not enjoy unconditional freedom, it is because we have limited our consciousness, not because consciousness has limited us. If we're aware only of our drama, pain, self-rejection, and problems, then that's what we see. As soon as we get above all this, we know that these concerns are not quite as meaningful as we thought they were.

The limitations we experience in our life are all self-imposed, and most of the time unconsciously. God does not limit us, nor does our partner or our boss. We do it. In order to grow, we have to affirm, "I'm conscious of the different dimensions within me and I have chosen to live in the deepest part of myself—in the depth of joy that is available to me—not in the suffering, limitation, or misunderstanding."

The option to be unhappy, to live in a very limited dimension, is always a choice. Conversely, viewing every situation in life as an opportunity to grow is also the result of a conscious decision to find a deeper place inside. We keep hoping that life will magically change, that angels will arrive and sprinkle fairy dust on us. But even if angels do appear, how often might we choose to wipe off the dust instead of absorb its energy?

We have to make important decisions about where we focus in life, and then find the strength to live up to our choices. That's what commitment is all about. It's like a tether that holds us when the winds blow. The commitment is never the issue. It's the test of the commitment that's really critical. We must say, "I will do this and I will hold on to my focus no matter what it costs me." The inspiration to make a commitment somehow gets diminished when the resistance to living up to it comes along. That's where real discipline is required.

Discipline is developed by doing, but often we don't follow through on our intentions. If we make a commitment and then falter, it's counterproductive to get caught up in the guilt of "I didn't do it, I should/shouldn't have, I'm not good enough." This kind of thinking simply adds more drama to the situation. Whenever we feel as if we've been knocked down by failing to hold on to our choice, we have to get back up and start again. We may get knocked about repeatedly. That's part of the process, and it's what tests our mettle. If we want a spiritual life, the highest commitment is to open our heart and never close it. If you make that commitment and spend the rest of your life working to keep your heart open, you will find your freedom. You will find God.

THE DIVINE TAPESTRY

We can think of our lives as a cosmic tapestry that God designs and we weave in order to attain our freedom. This Divine tapestry is woven with the threads of longing, effort, Grace, gratitude, devotion, and the willingness to serve and surrender. Those essential threads are the warp and weft that constitute the fabric of spiritual practice. What we produce is a magic carpet that can carry us on our journey back to God. We all get to weave our own Divine Life, but we must understand that although we are in control of the weave, the design is God's, not ours.

There is a style of rug in Indonesia called *ikat*. When master weavers in that tradition begin a new carpet they start without an apparent design, but every thread is pre-dyed. A few inches may be beige, and then the color may change to gold, then perhaps to red or orange. The colored threads are woven perfectly into place, giving form and clarity to the design. Similarly, as we weave our personal carpets with the threads given to us by the Divine, we gain an appreciation for the majesty of the design. We learn to trust the Designer and to surrender our incessant need to control.

How do we begin to weave a new life? The first thread in our tapestry is longing, the profound desire to know God. We put a lot of emphasis on cultivating longing, because it is what motivates us to engage in and maintain a serious spiritual practice. Rudi called this foundational thread "the wish to grow."

Many people ramble through life without any apparent sense of longing and then, in a moment of Grace, it appears. How or why this arousal happens is ultimately not relevant. It doesn't even matter when we have the inspiration.

Whether we start our spiritual practice from a place of deep suffering or from one of profound happiness, we always have the freedom to choose something higher. There are a million reasons why we come to the possibility of our own Divine Life, but the only reason we embrace it is because we deeply want it. We engage in a spiritual practice, or even read a book, because we have some longing that has begun to whisper within us. What do we do then? Kabir says to us:

Friend, hope for the Guest while you are alive.
Jump into experience while you are alive!
Think... and think... while you are alive.
What you call "salvation" belongs to the time before death.
If you don't break your ropes while you're alive,
do you think ghosts will do it after?
The idea that the soul will join with the ecstatic
just because the body is rotten—
that is all fantasy.
What is found now is found then.
If you find nothing now, you will simply end up
with an apartment in the City of Death.
If you make love with the divine, now, in the next life
you will have the face of satisfied desire.
So plunge into the truth, find out who the Teacher is,
believe in the Great Sound!

If we truly wish to live in freedom, we must come to understand that there is no duality in existence. It is possible to experience the unity of all life and to be fully engaged with this incredible manifestation, instead of experiencing it as a field that pulls us out of ourselves. Spirituality is gaining freedom from our mistaken separate identity, and we accomplish that not only in meditation but through the celebration of our lives. We only need to stay centered in our hearts and not forget that our life is a reflection of an immutable place within ourselves, which is not affected by anything we create or experience.

Kundalini Sadhana:
A Path to Liberation

3

CHAPTER THREE

Kuṇḍalinī sādhana is the spiritual practice from which the Tantric Shaivite and Tantric Buddhist traditions emerged. It is a yogic system aimed at transforming our understanding of the three elements of our existence: body, mind, and Spirit. The practice of *Kuṇḍalinī* Yoga explores *Kuṇḍalinī* energy (Śakti), and develops the awareness of this energy to such a point that it may be grasped not only as the power of the individual self, but also as the fundamental power of the infinite Self, the Source of everything.

Kuṇḍalinī is the energy of life, or the Divine, as it is experienced in the individual. It is the energy and power of Consciousness, the vital force that gives life to the universe. We are not separate from or different from that Source. *Kuṇḍalinī* is traditionally represented as a coiled serpent in the *cakra* at the base of the spine, and the three coils of the serpent represent:

- *Prāṇa-Kuṇḍalinī*
  the energy that gives life to the physical body
- *Cit-Kuṇḍalinī*
  the energy of our mind and emotions
- *Parā-Kuṇḍalinī*
  the energy of our spiritual Self

Parā-Kuṇḍalinī, the highest level of creative energy, is often referred to as existing in a dormant state in the base of the spine. The *Cit* and *Prāṇa* levels are always functioning, giving life to our bodies, thoughts, and emotions. What is hidden from us is the understanding that we are not different from our Divine Source, and that profound realization lies within the sleeping (*Parā*) *Kuṇḍalinī*. It is not really dormant so much as we are not aware of it.

KUNDALINI AS A FORCE WITHIN US

Kuṇḍalinī is not just the energy of the *cakra* located at the base of the spine. It is much more than that. *Kuṇḍalinī* is the power that gives life to everything, as well as the power that frees us. It is the rising of the *Kuṇḍalinī* from the base of the spine, piercing and releasing the awareness within each *cakra*, which cuts through our tensions, blocks, ignorance, and ego. Although *Kuṇḍalinī* is the energy of the Divine as it is experienced in the individual, it binds us when we project its energy into the world without remaining in our center. It is only when we return this energy inward to its Divine origin that *Kuṇḍalinī* has the ability to liberate us.

In order to activate the rising of the *Kuṇḍalinī* we must deeply open our hearts, inviting higher energies into our *cakras*, the psychic mechanism within us. Gradually, we develop a conscious flow of spiritual forces within. Flow is at once the breath, the underlying energy of that breath, and the emergent resonance we feel when all of the *cakras* are opened and the spiritual energies within them are released—allowing them to resonate with the descending spiritual forces that exist all around us.

Flow is energy in motion when we are completely open. When sound moves through the atmosphere it does so on energy that is projected ahead of it, creating the pathway on which the sound travels. In the same way, flow purifies the psychic channels within us, enabling the *Kuṇḍalinī* to rise. It is the energetic highway on which our consciousness travels.

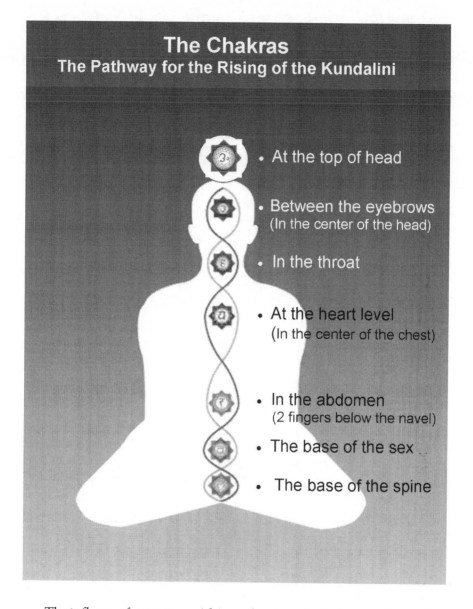

The Chakras
The Pathway for the Rising of the Kundalini

- At the top of head

- Between the eyebrows
  (In the center of the head)

- In the throat

- At the heart level
  (In the center of the chest)

- In the abdomen
  (2 fingers below the navel)

- The base of the sex

- The base of the spine

That flow of energy within a human is but one dimension expressed by the *Kuṇḍalinī*. There is really only One Energy in the universe—a central energy that functions in and supports all dimensions of existence. Śakti is the creative power of Śiva's Consciousness, the Source from which all manifestation appears. In relationship to *Kuṇḍalinī* and flow, the *Parā-Kuṇḍalinī* is pure potential, like a river with a dam holding the water back. The river becomes a reservoir, and has potential energy that is restrained from flowing. Flow is when the river runs through a channel (the psychic mechanism) and becomes an active energy of motion. The potential energy (*Parā-Kuṇḍalinī*) and the energy in motion (flow) are the same energy. It is the flow that opens up the pathway for the full force and potential of the *Kuṇḍalinī* to express itself in our lives.

By tuning in to that flow and consciously bringing it down to the base of the spine, we begin to awaken the highest aspect of *Kuṇḍalinī*, facilitating its rise toward the top of the head. That energy moves up through our subtle body, piercing the *cakras* and *granthi*—the dense gnarls that are the three major psychic knots within us. These knots are crystallized contractions, conjunctions of lifetimes of tension, pattern, psychic trauma, and ego. They coalesce around the *cakras* in the base of the spine, the heart, and the center of the head, blinding us to the intrinsic consciousness within.

One cannot find these knots in the body, nor do we need to. Instead, we focus on the flow of the vital force within. That energy works like an effervescent, dissolving tensions and contractions as it moves through the *cakras*, ultimately piercing the knots and releasing the consciousness bound within them. It is this breaking through the knots that allows the *Kuṇḍalinī* to rise and reunite with Pure Consciousness. This happens in the center of the head and in the *sahasrāra* (crown of the head)—which are in essence one space, what Bhagavan Nityananda called "the sky of the heart." When that occurs we achieve our realization and freedom.

FROM DUALITY TO UNITY

This profound transformation is palpable and definable in terms of our individual experience. It is nothing less than the transformation of individual experience and awareness from the mundane to the Divine, from duality to Unity. This is the progression of our individuated experience, which starts with diversity (duality), moves to understanding the Unity within the diversity, and finally to complete Unity.

The breaking of the knots corresponds directly to these stages of our experience:

- Diversity – *The duality in which we experience ourselves as separate from the Divine.*
  - Until the knot in the base of the spine is broken we live entirely in a dualistic experience. Our life force is projected completely outward.
  - Once that knot is broken we can begin to have glimpses of life other than the limited "there is me and there is everything else" experience.
  - We begin to open up inside.
- Unity in Diversity – *When the knot in the heart dissolves, we experience the Divine.*
  - Our experience shifts from being bound by a limited understanding of duality to recognizing the Oneness of life. Our life force turns within.
  - While we still experience all of the diversity, we understand that diversity to be part the whole.
  - We experience life as a flow.
- Complete Unity – *When the knot in the center of the head is broken through, we are completely immersed into the Divine.*
  - All of creation, although multifaceted, is experienced as an expression of the life force.
  - Our experience in and of life is one of witnessing complete harmony and Unity.
  - We live in a state of surrender.

While it is possible for a person to have an instant awakening, it is much more common for realization to come gradually.

Disciplined inner work, practiced in depth over time, gives us glimpses of our own Divinity, inspiring an ever-deepening wish to transform our experience and consciousness. By opening our hearts and cultivating flow, we are awakening the vital force within. *Kuṇḍalinī* rises up to pierce the *cakras* and cut through the psychic knots, allowing our true nature to reveal itself. When the *Kuṇḍalinī* is fully awakened we experience the complete unity of life.

BREATH, CHAKRA, FLOW, PRESENCE

My teacher Swami Chetanananda often used those words to describe the progression of the awakening of the *Kuṇḍalinī*. It eloquently describes the transformation of our experience and consciousness through the practice of *Kuṇḍalinī* Yoga. This sequence of words elucidates the inner practice of reaching inside with our breath, coming in contact with the energy that gave us life, and discovering the source of that energy, which is Presence, or Supreme Consciousness, beautifully expressing the movement from duality to Unity.

"Breath, *Cakra*, Flow, Presence" also succinctly describes the experience we seek as a spiritual person—in meditation, throughout our day, and in the course of our life—as we move toward the recognition that we are not separate from Oneness. This progression unfolds as we activate and awaken the *Kuṇḍalinī* within us.

Every time we sit down to meditate we should be attempting to shift our consciousness. As we follow the sequence of attaching our awareness to our breath, bringing our attention inside, opening the *cakras*, and feeling the flow, we are expanding the *suṣumṇa* (sushumna, or central channel) and allowing the vital force within us to rise back up and merge with Consciousness in the *sahasrāra*, where we experience Presence.

As we move off of our cushion and engage the world every day, the same progression is consciously repeated. We participate in life, with all of its diversity, but when we use our breath to connect to and open our *cakras*, releasing the flow within, we are then able to remain in our center at all times. When we engage in the world from that place, everything is transformed into energy and flow, and we can then use that energy to uncover a deeper consciousness, from which we experience the world and ourselves as One Thing, as Unity—the emergent quality of Presence.

From the perspective of our life span, the first thing we experience in birth is breath. Later, we become aware that our breath is not just an involuntary impulse of the physical body but also serves as our pathway to becoming more conscious. By deeply connecting to our breath, we can tune in to the source of that breath inside us. Through activating the *cakras* we are getting in touch with the vibrant power of life and allowing the flow of that effulgent force to show us the depth of our own life. We experience the blossoming of that flow into a state of Presence, of permanent unity with God. And just as our first breath emerges out of Presence, true liberation happens as our last breath merges back into That.

POWERFUL TECHNIQUES FOR AWAKENING THE KUNDALINI

In practicing *Kuṇḍalinī sādhana* we use a number of techniques to tune our awareness to a deeper place within and to extend that inner experience out into our daily life. Many of the discussions that follow will refer to some important practices, primarily Rudi's double-breath exercise and a method for releasing negative psychic tensions. It will be helpful for the reader to have some familiarity with these techniques. A written description of them is provided on the following pages.

DOUBLE-BREATH EXERCISE

The double-breath exercise developed by Swami Rudrananda is a very important tool for meditation. It will help you to experience and deepen the flow of vital force. The double-breath integrates the wish to grow with awareness of the breath, the *cakras*, and the flow of energy within, all into one smooth process. With the double-breath, you are working to establish a flow of energy down the front and up the back. Use the double-breath every ten minutes during meditation to sharpen your inner focus. Use it throughout the day.

1. Take a deep breath, let it go, and relax.
2. Be aware that the breath is filled with spiritual energy and nourishment.
3. Draw the next breath into the heart *cakra*. As the breath moves through the throat *cakra*, swallow. Without forcing the breath, allow it to fill and open your chest. Relax in the heart *cakra* and feel an expansion taking place. Feel a deep wish to grow. Ask deeply to open your heart; ask deeply to surrender your worries, problems, and boundaries. Hold the breath in the heart for about ten seconds or until it naturally releases.
4. Release about one-fifth of the breath and deeply let go. Keep your attention and energy in your heart.
5. Breathe in again, through the heart, bringing the breath and your attention into the navel *cakra*. Hold gently and relax deeply. Feel your belly open and soften with the expansion of energy. Hold the breath and your attention there for about ten seconds. As you release the breath, feel the energy naturally expand across the sex *cakra* and into the base of the spine.

6. Relax the base of the spine and allow the energy to rise up the spinal column to the top of the head. Feel the energy there.

At other times during meditation, when not doing the double-breath, remain very aware of your breath, and focus your breath and attention on the heart *cakra*. Be aware of the flow of energy moving down through the *cakras* and up the spinal column to the top of the head. At the end of each outbreath, let go, and then let go again. Feel the expansion in yourself. Surrender inside, allowing something deeper and finer to fill you. It is this ever-deepening practice that mobilizes your inner energy to facilitate a very profound and lasting change in your consciousness and in your experience of life.

TENSION RELEASE EXERCISE

This is an excellent tool for letting go of the tensions we accumulate during our day or during a powerful period in our lives. It is also a very effective means of flushing out the energetic residue from our meditation practice. Activating the flow of *Kundalinī* will break up any barriers or crystallized energy present inside, and it is then important to release what we have just dislodged from our system.

Doing this exercise releases that negative psychic tension in our internal channel, allowing for a greater openness and more powerful flow. Try to do this exercise at least once a day, for fifteen to twenty minutes.

1. Close your eyes, relax, get in touch with your breath. Breathe easily and deeply, relaxing fully. Let your arms hang down at your sides away from your body, or over the arms of your chair.

2. Focus your attention on your heart *cakra* and ask to release all tensions. Ask to release the negative psychic tensions and energetic residue, the contraction and thickness inside. Feel the tensions releasing from your midsection and heart. Feel it move out to your shoulders, down your arms, and out of your hands.

3. Shake your hands periodically to throw off the released tensions.

For readers wishing to incorporate these exercises in their lives, guided meditations are available as a resource at *TrikaShala.com*. Open the Writings & Photos page from the left-side menu. Then click on the Guided Meditation link under Swami Khecaranatha's name. When prompted, enter the password RUDRA. This will take you to a page with the MP3 files.

There is no cost for this, and I encourage you to begin using these meditation techniques as you continue to read this book. I offer these techniques because they are an integral part of this practice, but I recognize that some readers may already be engaged in other types of meditation. Ultimately, the specific techniques you use are not important—as long as they give you access to the vital force within you.

ACCESSING THE POWER OF KUNDALINI

The use of the double-breath allows us to draw in nourishment from the power of *Kuṇḍalinī* within ourselves and life around us. Be very clear that the energy is the same. There is really no inside energy or outside energy. Developing a conscious flow within yourself will reveal that understanding by means of your own direct experience of working with this spiritual energy. This process of drawing in nourishment starts to dissolve the blocks in our psychic mechanism.

What happens to us sometimes is that we take a breath, don't feel anything, and think the technique doesn't work. And really, it doesn't—unless we take the next breath, and the next breath, and keep feeling inside, and feeling underneath our matchbox-sized heart, and begin to really resonate with that vital force.

We attach our attention to that breath, we breathe inside, begin to feel the *cakras*, and create a flow within us. The flow is the resonance when all of the *cakras* are open. It is the resonance of the force within that is ascending from the *cakras* and our connection to descending spiritual forces. Opening the *cakras* gives us access to flow, and that flow is what washes away all tension, ego, victim-consciousness, and all worry about "What's going to happen to me?"

If we put one-billionth of the energy that we invest in sustaining our dramas into simply opening our heart and feeling a flow, we would have extraordinary transformation in our lives. It is the development of the conscious flow that gives us access to deeper awareness within. This process is like dripping water on something solid. Over time, it starts to soften and dissolve. It is our conscious choice to bring that energy in and wake the Goddess Kundalinī (*Parā-Kundalinī*)—to enliven Her energy and allow Her to rise and merge back into Śiva, the seat of consciousness within a human being. It is that re-merging that is the essence of the practice of *Kundalinī* Yoga.

The base of the spine is the bedroom where the Goddess "sleeps," encased in a shell. Our daily morning delivery of croissants and café au lait awakens Her, and slowly, the vital force from within us begins to move up. There is a softening of the shell, and small bits of it start to release and dissolve. When we feel that release, it is the result of the energy we are moving up from the base of the spine to the top of the head. That flow of vital force is now rising through our psychic system. People often think that the initial stirring of *Kundalinī* energy, the feeling of it moving up from the base of the spine, is a state of awakened *Kuṇḍalinī*. But this is just the beginning of a process of our *Kuṇḍalinī* awakening.

As I've said previously, we can think of that dormant vital force within as being like the water behind a dam. There is a powerful pure potential there. The water is tremendously deep, and while it looks still, there is a pulsation moving against the boundary, ready to move. When the floodgates are opened there is enormous power, enormous movement of flow. And so it is with the *Kuṇḍalinī* energy—that dormant force in a human being contains an extraordinary power and potential that is just waiting to be released within us.

The release, the opening of the gates, is the opening of the psychic body. As that energy begins to move, its force washes away anything that blocks its path. It grows, it gets bigger, and like the power of a river, it clears out all impediments in its way.

A dammed river is never diminished in its capacity or in its power. It is just held back. This is what happens in us as humans. As we consciously open the gates, the flow begins to uncover all our potential and express itself as a whole new vibrancy. The wonderful part of this analogy is that all great rivers flow into the ocean. As we release this power of the Goddess within us, She moves up through our psychic system, pierces all the *cakras*, releases all barriers and all wisdom, and ultimately reemerges into the infinite ocean of Consciousness.

FLOW HAPPENS IN A VERTICAL AND HORIZONTAL MATRIX

The conscious discipline of developing a flow and extending it into our daily life is a vital element of *Kuṇḍalinī* Yoga. Flow happens as a matrix of the vertical and horizontal.

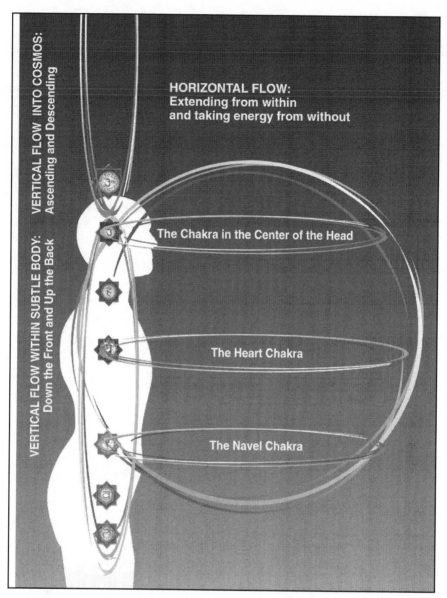

VERTICAL FLOW INTO COSMOS:
Ascending and Descending

VERTICAL FLOW WITHIN SUBTLE BODY:
Down the Front and Up the Back

HORIZONTAL FLOW:
Extending from within
and taking energy from without

The Chakra in the Center of the Head

The Heart Chakra

The Navel Chakra

Vertical can be described as being the flow that moves within our psychic body—up the *suṣumṇa*, out the top of the head, connecting us to the cosmos, and then back down into us. Horizontal flow is that which moves out from the inner flow, extending into our life in the world. It is actually this horizontal flow that creates our life and our world. However, it's important to understand that in reality there is only One Energy, permeating everything, everywhere. There is no up, down, in, or out.

So which comes first, the vertical or the horizontal flow? Of course that's a trick question, because life doesn't happen in one dimension of the matrix—it happens in all dimensions simultaneously. Both the inner and outer flows are part of one energy field, part of the creation that emerges from Supreme Consciousness. Having a living experience of this dynamic is what dissolves duality, and coming to the understanding of how the energy of life functions in all dimensions on the field of Consciousness is integral to the practice of *Kuṇḍalinī* Yoga.

THE WORK OF ABSORBING ENERGY

The internal vertical flow that we create must be extended from our center, from our heart, to connect with the energy around us. As soon as we understand that the manifest world is simply energy—that it is not somebody or something—we can feel it and interact with it in a fundamentally different way. What we initially think of as external energy is not different from the energy within us. It may, however, appear different in the beginning. Someone else's contraction may feel like tension, but if we keep reaching into it, suddenly, it doesn't feel like tension anymore. When we understand that tension is just energy that is contracted or not in motion, our relationship to it has changed. The other person may or may not share this understanding, but that is not relevant to our own experience.

Changing our experience is a lot of work, and it requires a daily effort of getting conscious, being knocked unconscious by the dynamics that we engage in, and then throwing some water on our face to revive ourselves. We do this time after time, until we really learn to relate to everything as energy that we can put into the flow. We discover that we are always engaging the one creative force as it manifests as all the aspects of our life. What makes this easier is not labeling the energy and categorizing it as some form.

As that energy within us rises, it exposes a bigger consciousness from which we can then re-engage life. We then function from a completely different consciousness, transcending the misunderstanding that the dynamic we are involved in is about somebody or something else. We understand that all life and all activity is not about form but energy — and this energy can be used to transform our experience when we put that force into the flow within.

When we deeply open and begin to establish this flow inside it creates the perfect situation for us to free ourselves from some powerful pattern or tension within. If we become tense, feel sorry for ourselves, or reject ourselves, we are only playing the game I call "Let's Get Tense." All of these reactions are an incorrect response to whatever situation was created by the flow itself, for the very purpose of exposing our limitations and giving us the opportunity of opening to a bigger place inside. What happens when we play Let's Get Tense? We contract, nothing flows, and we lose contact with our center. But if we remain conscious we can turn that contracted energy back into flow. Because flow is energy in motion, it has an infinite capacity to expand and dissolve the internal obstacle that created the contraction in the first place.

I saw a fabulous television program that dramatically illustrated how a conscious flow allows us to absorb and transmute any obstacle. One segment of the show was about a twenty-five-foot python that swallowed a deer. As the deer was drinking from a stream, the python grabbed it by the foot, and then wrapped itself around its prey to suffocate it. The python then proceeded to dislocate its jaw wide enough to get it around the carcass of the deer, swallowing it whole. At that point what we see is this huge python lying there with a big lump in the middle of it, slowly digesting that food. It doesn't have to eat for about two years after that! The process is not essentially different for us. When we encounter difficulty in life we must understand that it is just "lunch"—the very nourishment we need for our growth. We open bigger than the difficulty, absorbing and digesting the energy of it, thereby creating a bigger and stronger flow inside.

The symbol for *Kuṇḍalinī* Śakti is the serpent. This vital force will dislocate its jaw and it will consume us. *Kuṇḍalinī* consumes all of our patterns, tensions, contractions, and karma. What can we do when we have been swallowed by the python? Surrender. The smart *sādhaka* (spiritual student) drinks water from the edge of the river praying to be grabbed by the snake. Instead, we typically play the other game of life, which is called "Run Away . . . Keep Running."

We must allow *Kuṇḍalinī* to perform Her work. Flow is a conscious energy that we release from within ourselves and it has its own innate intelligence. It will consume all obstacles within us, liberating us in the process. The python analogy demonstrates not only our capacity to do the work of digesting energy, but also how the energy itself ultimately consumes us.

FREEING OURSELVES FROM OUR INTERIOR BLOCKS

As we establish a flow inside we expose the inner barriers blocking the further expansion of that flow. In traditional texts, these are called impurities—our thoughts, mind, and emotions, plus our contractions and patterns. This is what obstructs the flow. As the internal energetic floodgate is opened, the force of that flow meets any obstacles and exposes them. That is exactly what the flow is intended to do: to expose, unblock, and ultimately free us from all obstacles within. The reason the *Kuṇḍalinī* force appears to be dormant in us is that She is covered up by so much stuff that She has no oxygen. She can't breathe, so She passes out!

Our job is to uncover and remove the rubble inside us as quickly as possible, so that some oxygen begins to get to the Goddess. When miners get trapped in a shaft, the first thing rescuers do is drill a small hole into that area so that the men can get air. That is essentially what we are doing with our spiritual exercises. We create some movement and energy, allowing a trickle of nourishment into our system so that we can start to function. Once the Goddess Kuṇḍalinī begins to breathe, She stirs within us. She rolls over in Her sleep, wakes up a bit, and opens Her eyes for some time. As She starts to rise, Her energy is able to dissolve the barriers and release everything that suffocates our own true Self. It is the energy that does all the work. As it rises, it pierces the *cakras* and frees us from the true obstacles embedded within our psychic system—especially the ones lodged deeper than where we normally look.

THE MIND IS A THIEF

Śakti is the burning of lesser things. Developing the capacity to expose and burn our limitations is the result of creating the internal flow within ourselves. In Sanskrit the word for the burning that takes place as we do our *sādhana* is *tāpasya*, which refers to the internal fire that consumes any blocks in its path. Our spiritual work is not a game of bob and weave. We are not looking around the corner to see if one of our issues is going to be waiting there to get in our way. What we should be saying is, "Bring it on. Let's get the boulders out of the way."

We understand that flow is what is going to clear out all those obstacles, which is why we embrace every situation we encounter from a state of openness. Then all of the hard work of changing becomes a work of joy, of consciousness. Our work is one of facilitating the flow, which primarily means getting out of its way. Ultimately, the work we do is to surrender to the Goddess' will, to let Her power design our life in ways we cannot even imagine.

But there is a trick here, because the very power that exists within us, which will begin to free itself completely, has given us equal power to say no. And as more power is released within us, there is a greater and greater chance that the mind will become a thief. The mind says, "it is mine, all mine," and uses power for its own defense. Spiritual growth is therefore always a conscious path, requiring us to continuously choose between two things—being open or being closed. In its highest level, it's a choice between freedom and bondage.

KARMA IS WOOD FOR THE FIRE

When we say that our *Kuṇḍalinī* energy is in a dormant state, this does not mean She is unconscious within Herself, but only that we are unaware of Her. As they say, Hell has no wrath like that of a woman scorned! The Goddess is fully aware of *us* at all times, and when She rises, watch out. She is going to obliterate us—and that's a wonderful thing.

At a certain point, when the energy starts to intensify, our job is to sing, "Hit me with your best shot . . . Fire away . . ." and then not contract as that happens. We need to get past ourselves. All of the traumas, pain, and suffering we feel are completely real, but we can either get caught up in them or we can burn them and free ourselves.

Creating this flow exposes our karma. What is revealed are all the patterns of self-absorption and self-serving that we have created in this and past lifetimes. Those patterns are the coalescence of all our tensions, attachments, contractions, and resistance. That is what forces us to repeat the same thing, over and over again—usually projected at the world and the people in it. This is how we create karma.

The bumper sticker about karma reads: You Did It, Now Undo It. We must free ourselves from our karma. In order to do that, we have to work in the place from which the karma was created—but by relating to the dynamic as an energy field and not as a particular circumstance. When we find ourselves in a karmic relationship, we have to separate from the specifics of the engagement. We do this by recognizing that there is a pattern of energy in that situation which is trapped on the merry-go-round of our life. We understand what part of us created it, and ask, "How do I free myself of it?"

Freeing ourselves doesn't mean saying, "Okay, bye," and walking away. We can't just walk away from our karma. We can't escape it, nor should we want to, because there is tremendous energy and freedom available to us in liberating ourselves from karmic patterns and relationships. So many times those dynamics are really powerful and really painful.

If we are conscious, our karmic relationships will expose extraordinary limitations within us. If we are unconscious, we always believe our tensions and our contractions are someone else's fault!

What people do to us is their karma; how we react is ours. As this torrential flow of *śakti* is released within us, it exposes all misunderstanding, all limitation. We don't beat ourselves up because we have misunderstood. It's better to embrace our misconceptions so that we can be clear of them. We don't get involved and dramatic, but instead accept any revelation with an openness that expresses, "This is part of my limited understanding of the truth of life and I want it to be exposed. I want to burn it up in the fire of Consciousness."

FLOW MATURES INTO THE FLOWERING OF CONSCIOUSNESS

If we cannot flow with our life, we will never find flow in ourselves. If we cannot learn to have a dynamic interchange with the manifestation of life that has emerged from within us, we cannot reabsorb this energy back inside and into the vertical force that will uplift and free us. Flow can be defined as creation moving through us, and in order for creation to express itself fully, everything must be in the flow.

We all recognize the beauty and strength of a lotus flower. A lotus has a stem that projects about two feet out of the water and the flower blossoms on top. The analogy to spiritual practice is that the flower is supported by, and attached to, the scum at the bottom of the water. It is nourished by what is at the bottom, but it is untouched by it. This is why we often see the form of the lotus depicting the flowering of consciousness. What supports that unfoldment of consciousness is the flow of life, which includes even the densest, darkest, most buried parts of us. All energy held within us moves up our internal stem, the *suṣumṇa*.

The double-breath is an extremely powerful exercise for drawing our life force back into us. We pull that energy in through our psychic body instead of allowing it to be projected outside ourselves—where, before we even become aware, it's out beyond the stratosphere and on its way to Pluto. We must draw that force back in and return it to the place from which it came. The double-breath and the feeling of flow create what Rudi used to call "psychic Drano." This fantastic product cleans out all the debris within the *suṣumṇa*. And make no mistake: that debris is you. The blockage is our accumulated patterns, tensions, and karma. It is only after all the sludge has been removed that our awareness is transformed.

The raising of the *Kuṇḍalinī* is identical with the vertical flow, which does all the work of clearing out the *cakras*, thereby opening the *suṣumṇa*. It is when this channel has become purified—when there is a straight shot from the base of the spine to the center of the head—that the Goddess will rise. The Goddess is very smart and sends out scout ants in the form of energy in us, checking out the environment. It is only when the pathway is completely clear that She fully emerges.

The awakening and rising of *Kuṇḍalinī* is not symbolism. As we continually consume and reinvest the life force that is both creating us and manifesting through us, we experience flow maturing into a more refined and encompassing energy field. We begin to have the experience that every time we breathe, our entire life force is not only moving out the top of the head but also looping back around to the base of the spine and straight to the top of the head again. What has been created is a continuously deepening and expansive flow that we experience both inside and outside the physical body.

Eventually our experience changes: the energy still loops out the top of the head and back into the *suṣumṇa*, but not through the *cakra* at the base of the spine. The energy reenters us through the base of the spine in a completely different place, which is only revealed once this flow has freed us and burned through everything that had previously obscured it. This purification uncovers a new doorway—a stillpoint in the center of the *suṣumṇa* at the base of the spine. When the flow is able to reenter us through that stillpoint, what we experience is that there are no *cakras*. There is only a pure light, a pure tube with no obstruction, which serves as a conduit for that Divine Force to rise and to reemerge and unify back into its own Source.

The eleventh-century Tantric Shaivite text Yogini Hrdayam beautifully describes this experience: "Recognize the Goddess as pure light, which emanates and creates from within the *suṣumṇa* and creates you." The *suṣumṇa* is the pure light from which we are formed. Direct experience of our Source unfolds with the flowering of consciousness. That is why I talk about breath, *cakra*, flow, Presence. That Presence is the "pure light" referred to in the Yogini Hrdayam.

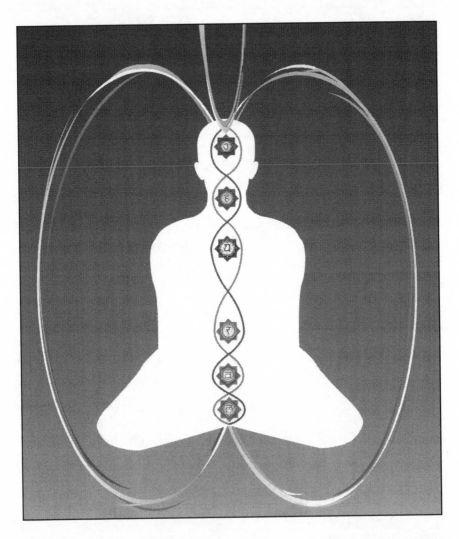

It is when—through the power of flow—our life force has been purified and completely reinvested within that we will have our experience of liberation, of permanently merging with the highest Consciousness. This is why the power of flow is the gift of life.

WE EMERGE AS INDIVIDUALS AS A STREAK OF LIGHT

To further illustrate the nature of this pure light and energy, I would like to paraphrase a section from a book entitled *Stillness* written by Charles Ridley. He wrote that modern medicine has now demonstrated that in the first two weeks following conception, the embryo is amorphous protoplasm. It possesses no structure but is simply a clear-as-glass liquid crystal matrix. Then, on day fourteen, it begins to organize cells that produce a visible line in the embryo, called the primitive streak, or the midline (the *suṣumṇa*). The core of that midline is stillness or Presence.

Enfolded within that is a holographic electromagnetic (energy) field, and it is from this field that the development of the human being takes place. From this primitive streak of light, an invisible line transforms into a visible line and becomes the core around which a human being is created. Arising out of that streak, like branches from a tree trunk, emerge all aspects of the human being. Essentially, the progression is from the original primitive streak (as invisible stillness), to an eminence of light, which in turn manifests as form.

This description provides a powerful understanding of how we become an individuated expression of the Divine—of how we emerge from essence, from Consciousness, from pure light, from *Kuṇḍalinī*.

THE INFINITE FLOW OF OPENNESS

What we're trying to establish in ourselves is a flow of openness—and the bigger the openness, the bigger the energy . . . and the bigger the energy, the bigger the openness. So don't get caught in the idea of a *cakra* as a fixed point, or try to uncover the exact qualities of one versus another. What we're looking for is the flow created when all the *cakras* open and are humming together.

We may feel something move between one *cakra* and another, and that's good because it's evidence that the energy is moving. But the flow I'm talking about only happens when we've opened up deeply enough, and let go of enough of our baggage for a sufficient length of time, to enable these *cakras* to be in a state of permanent openness. That's when the energy can continually flow through us.

Flow ultimately brings us into pure Presence without us ever losing contact with the movement of that vital force. We then discover that inside Presence is yet another power of flow, which opens up and expands again. Growth is never ending. How can you mark an end to the infinite? Energy rises, consciousness expands. That is the matrix of the horizontal and the vertical, which continues throughout our life.

The purpose of life is liberation; it's about being freed from our limited self. All of life arises from Consciousness, and it manifests and is created through the matrix of energy. We too are an expression of this creative manifestation of force, and what we're attempting to do is return back to that Consciousness. That's where realization is found.

All the techniques and all the endless turmoil we go through in our *sādhana* are just what we go through in the process. Don't focus on that. Focus on what you're asking to have happen in you by taking your energy inside, opening your heart, and, from that place, deeply asking to open again. Understand the profound transformation available when you surrender to the vital force within you.

Without a doubt one of the most significant aspects of that transformation is coming in contact with Divine Love. This happens as we move into Presence, and as the flow within us tunes our mechanism so that it can resonate to the same frequency of the subtle Divine Love that is expressing all life. Divine Love is always present in our lives. There is never a moment in which that love is not available to us. It is the flow which moves us into that experience and then gives us the capacity to express unconditional love—the perfection of flow.

CONNECTING WITH A HIGHER POWER

When we create this internal flow, we are tapping into the higher power of God, a "descending force" we consciously draw inside. This energy gives us sustenance and the needed fuel for growth. As Rudi put it, we do this work "to nourish those thousands of psychic muscles within and begin to give them functionality." After we bring this force down to the base of the spine, we allow it to rise back up and out the top of the head, completing the circuit. We are, in effect, internalizing the energy and then sending it back to God. We are creating a vertical flow in the form of a Divine thread that connects us to God. That is, in its simplest essence, the practice that brings us liberation.

In the beginning of our practice if feels as if we have to reach outside ourselves to find that which is already inside. We connect to a higher descending force, pull it in as nourishment, and bring it down to the base of the spine. There, the descending energy meets with the same vital force, already present within us. We feed this inner place, which releases energy upward, so that it can rise back to meet the very same Source "outside of us."

This discussion reveals the importance of freeing ourselves from dualistic perception, because the question arises: "Is this vital force outside or inside of us? Is it above us, or is it in the base of the spine?" We are immediately confronted with our view of reality, which is locked in the misconception that there are two things—us and some God above. This apparent paradox provides a perfect lesson, because the brain needs to receive the message of Unity again and again in order to get the point. We have to hear it, see it, feel it, and be smashed and caressed by it a million times before the density of our dualistic misunderstanding can really start to dissolve. So even at the very beginning, when Unity is not our experience, we must reach to comprehend and embrace it.

As we create this vertical flow inside, our experience of it changes as we become more adept at tuning in to the *cakras*. By repeatedly working within, we learn how to really feel what is there. Some people have a great sense of the visual, others rely more on sound. Both are described in the ancient texts as totally valid means of perception.

Feeling the *cakras* is ultimately a matter of experiencing them as a distinct resonance in ourselves. When we bring our attention inside and are able to feel the awareness and energy within each *cakra* open, we gain a completely different level of perception—one that releases an understanding beyond what we might anticipate. It's like opening a door to reveal a view of something we could not even imagine from the other side.

Having a connection to God, or a higher force, is literally experienced through flow. As we master the capacity to open all of the *cakras*, our experience is that flow, at its purest, has no constriction. The current that moves through us is as real and palpable as sticking a finger in a wall socket. *Kuṇḍalinī sādhana* enables us to develop the mastery, the sensitivity, to feel this flow within, to become established within it, and to allow it to transform and free us.

SHIFTING TO OPENNESS

The first experience of freedom is an open heart, an internal expansiveness. There is a shift from one state of awareness to another—from worrying about the dramas and challenges of our lives to a focus on openness, clarity, and stillness. Every time we meditate, we are seeking to move from tightness to expansiveness. Once that shift has happened, we get up, engage with our day, and take care of our responsibilities. Spiritual development does not mean spacing out all day. If we want freedom, we must develop the ability to feel the flow as we move through our lives.

Every one of us has had the experience that when we are bothered by something, it feels like a splinter in our finger which is irritated and swelling. That aggravation is all we can keep our attention on, and it becomes the focus of our experience. On the other hand, when we wake up in the morning and that drop of *rasa,* or essence, is soothing us, then that is what we bring to our day. Whatever we find within ourselves is the expression and the experience of our life. We have the power to either get caught up in the festering of the splinter or to simply tune in to the *rasa.* When we realize that life happens from within us—not to us— we gain the capacity to choose our experience by focusing on openness and freedom.

Think about your own life. Think about the lives and the choices of the people you know. What are we normally trying to do? We attempt to change how life manifests in order to change our experience. Day after day, we take a sledgehammer to life, trying to sculpt it into our image of perfection, our image of what we think we must have in order to be happy. What if we took the opposite approach? Master sculptor Michelangelo said that the finished statue is already present inside a block of stone, and he let the stone reveal the hidden form. He accepted what was inside a particular piece of marble, rather than taking a chisel and trying to force it into something other than what it was. Isn't that wonderful?

CHANGING OUR EXPERIENCE OF THE WORLD

In this dance of creation, it is our inner mastery—our inner experience of life—that decides whether or not we are free. We don't need to change the world or the conditions we encounter in order to experience our own true nature. We must stop trying to change that which probably doesn't need to be changed in the first place. It is only our arrogance that decides something should be different.

God gives us exactly what we need in each moment. Our life is expressing itself perfectly from within us, but what do we do? We start trying to change our life, based on our limited perception of what we think we need or want. Once we go inside and recognize the Source of all manifestation, we immediately have the experience that our life is perfect right now, as it is. We no longer have the need to try to change anything except our own perception.

If we really want to change our life, we need to change our consciousness. What is critical is our willingness and ability to reach past all of our emotions to find a deeper awareness. We take the energy that is contracted in a particular experience of jealousy, anger, or grief, and draw it back inside. The dense, stuck energy is thereby transmuted into something that can feed our awareness and flow, further strengthening the capacity to connect with our Source.

This is the inner discipline required to become a master of oneself, and if we create that capacity, what we express in our life is an effortless reflection of what we have found inside. We no longer need to blame somebody else or some other thing for the quality of our experience. We accept the responsibility because we have learned that we get to create our own experience.

The practice of *Kuṇḍalinī* Yoga has such a profound, extraordinary capacity to allow us to meet our day and consume the tensions of our life. This is why I often call the practice "The *Kuṇḍalinī* Kitchen: Where you cook your own soup." Even when it is somebody else's tension, it becomes ours if we allow it to contract us. There is no energy that we cannot open to, consume, pour into the flow, and thereby transform its density, this apparent block, into nourishment.

We can only love God from a place of freedom, and we create that freedom within ourselves by gaining the ability to be open and flow with every dynamic that life presents to us. We have to develop these psychic muscles through our inner practice—a practice that happens both in meditation and during our day.

We take the crudeness and the density of our life, and we refine that energy. As our awareness rises, the denser energies that used to stick to us just can't connect or hold on. They are still there, but we can now transcend them. Transcendence is a very real, conscious transformation of our awareness. It is different from sublimation or denial. With an open heart, every kind of dense energy within us gets broken down, so that the conscious person does not feel constricted and does not act from a place of limitation.

BORROW THE FLOW OF THE TEACHER

If you are in a *Kuṇḍalinī* Yoga meditation practice, you most likely have a teacher. The transmission of *śaktipāta*, the flow from teacher to student, is the essence of the practice—and this is certainly one of the most palpable and direct forms of receiving Grace. Any Tantric teaching would say that we cannot awaken our own *Kuṇḍalinī*. That power is within us, but it is so buried and our ego is so thick that we have little chance to uncover that inner force. There are certainly rare people who are born with an awakened *Kuṇḍalinī*, but this is far from usual.

Śaktipāta is the descent of Grace. The transmission of that Grace happens through look, touch, word, or thought—and this energy is the transforming agent in our life. It is the flow of Grace that can cut through any level of density within us, greatly augmenting whatever inner work we do on our own. That Divine nourishment feeds the Divinity within, allowing it to emerge and reveal itself to us. *Śaktipāta* is love freely given, a living spiritual force that not only opens the door within us but provides the nourishment and support necessary to keep that door open.

The ancient Tantric texts describe twenty-seven levels of transmission. Twenty-seven is what you get by multiplying nine degrees of *śaktipāta* by the three levels that are really important. (These ancient sages couldn't surf the Internet, so they had too much time on their hands!)

The three important levels of *śaktipāta* are:

- Direct transmission from the Goddess. We see this in the rare people who are born realized (what is called being an *avadhūta* in Sanskrit). These people have been directly touched by the Goddess Kuṇḍalinī without any human intermediary.
- Transmission through a teacher.
- The awakening of the wish within that eventually brings someone to a teacher.

An individual's karma creates the opportunity to receive the second level of *śaktipāta*, that of being touched by an adept. *Śaktipāta* is Grace—the freedom-bestowing power of the Divine. It is Divinity Itself that grants freedom, and our response should only be to receive, surrender, and accept. The purest form of flow in us is receiving, and once we have received that gift, our life has the possibility of immediate, radical transformation in every moment, from that point on. Not everyone on earth comes in contact with that level of Grace. If you have this opportunity in your life, be grateful.

Extraordinary growth happens when we open to receive the love and spiritual nourishment given by a teacher. *Śaktipāta* helps to break down misunderstanding within us, but because the purpose of the teacher is to free us, sometimes the interaction doesn't exactly come in a form that is easy to take. The teacher is a field of energy that will help burn up tensions and blocks within the student. We can think of the teacher as the fire that ignites the vital energy within a student—but it is the student who gets "cooked" from the inside out. When it is time to have part of us diced up to add to the soup, the teacher's job is to turn up the heat, not to pull us out of the pot!

So, the issue comes back to our own simple responsibility. What are we going to do with the Grace of our life? Reject it, because we are too involved in our personal trip? Reject it, because we want to play Let's Get Tense? If we really open up, that energy will free us. But in order for that to happen, we must surrender everything that gets in the way of transformation. Everything. Not some of it—everything. Our own gift of consciousness is to be able to say, "Yes, I am in my way. I am not willing to change. I am holding on, I am living in this fear, I need to control . . ." and then let go. The fastest way to burn through all limitation is to surrender your life to God. Are you prepared to do so? Maybe the real question is, *when* will you be prepared to do so?

Understand that every student will be tested. If we don't break down the deep levels of resistance within us, we will never get to reach into and access the Self. The connection to the vital force of the teacher is critical in breaking down our resistance. We are using the teacher to fan the flames of our own fire. It is only when we no longer need this energy that we no longer need a teacher. Later in the book we will explore the student-teacher relationship in depth.

BEING WILLING TO CHANGE

What do we do with the Grace we receive from the teacher? So much of the time, when we receive something that can truly free us, we try to give it back—often because we cannot imagine what it is trying to bring us. Even if we do have some idea, we still may not be willing to change. It really doesn't matter why we reject the gift. The subtlest effect of Grace is to free us from the very things we have no clue are binding us. We must profoundly believe that liberation is possible for us, and demand that in this life we receive the love and the freedom that we deserve.

The force that gives us life in our mother's womb cannot, and would not, abandon us after we are born. Yet because of the strength of the ego, we attempt to alter the design of the tapestry of our life. We keep trying to change or reject what is unfolding, thinking the design does not work for us. First, we blame those around us, and then we start blaming God. It is amazing to witness our inability to accept how Divine Grace manifests in our lives.

We have to trust in God and trust the Divine Force within that is trying to express Itself. The part of us that knows it is not separate from its own Source is trying to free us from our limited self. We must transcend the thinnest veil of the ego, which does not even know it is binding us. The ego is convinced, absolutely convinced, that it is a separate entity at the center of the universe, and that everything revolves around it. Isn't that how we walk through our day? What part of ourselves are we listening to? What part of ourselves do we trust?

Yes, it can be painful to let go of egoic thinking and self-centeredness, but how can we expect to receive the greatest treasure that exists, and not pay a little? We get what we demand in ourselves, and what we know we deserve. If we know we deserve liberation, we are willing to pay for it. The most beautiful words I have read about this come at the end of a Sufi poem: "I offer myself to God, without thought of price, to do with as He pleases." That expresses the ultimate trust and moves us into a discussion of gratitude and surrender.

Understanding Gratitude and Surrender

Surrender can be boiled down to one definition: the capacity and the willingness to be changed. It is the conscious act of letting go of whatever is within us that we can't shake off. There can never be anything negative in this because even if we are engaged in a difficult situation, if we approach it from a state of surrender we are freeing ourselves. We are learning, and we are being given the gift of that challenge.

Surrender results in the dissolution of our limited self. We let go of our separateness, our boundaries, and our deep attachment to our limitations. Because we get caught in the dualistic part of the world that expresses itself as the dynamics in our life, that arena is where the need to surrender plays itself out. The real issue, however, is never the dynamics themselves but rather the capacity to surrender our separateness from our own Source.

All situations in which we find ourselves, in which we are asked to surrender, are practice, only practice, for that moment of letting go and being immersed in our own Divinity. That is realization—the complete immersion into the entire unity of life. In that state there is only the experience of Oneness, and it takes a great depth of surrender to reach that level of consciousness. Remember, it is building a strong flow within ourselves that gives us the strength and capacity to surrender.

Rumi says, "There is one thing in this world you must never forget to do. If you forget everything else and not this, there's nothing to worry about, but if you remember everything else and forget this, then you will have done nothing in your life." How wonderfully said. We should live in the fullness of life—and that means we do not have to deny ourselves anything except that which keeps us from that effulgence. We must have the courage to ask ourselves, "What is the most important thing in my life?" And then we must develop the capacity to let go of those things we know are keeping us from that fullness. We must have the courage to trust God, and we must have the courage to be loved. We must live in gratitude for the joy of being loved by God.

EXTENDING INNER PRACTICE OUT INTO OUR LIVES

Freedom is the individuated experience of our own Divinity, but ultimately we discover that we are not individuals. In meditation we seek to shift our awareness so that our separateness dissolves. We want to experience Divinity in a state of stillness and awareness. This perceptual shift requires subtle awareness.

The purpose of meditation is not to get over our busy mind or our emotional trauma. The tensions of daily life should not be brought into meditation, but if we need to spend a few seconds getting over our mental busyness, so be it. We shouldn't just come to meditation to open our heart; rather, we should bring an open heart to our meditation. There is a profound difference between these two attitudes, and as we move from being amateurs in our practice to becoming professionals, we understand that distinction.

Shifting our awareness in meditation is only the beginning of our practice. Spiritual growth means deeply surrendering to a place of openness inside, and allowing it to emerge and fill our consciousness. It is from this fullness that we embrace and engage the world. Whether it takes twenty minutes or two hours to find that inner place, make sure that you do so on a regular basis. It is the ability to experience that infinite space within that allows us to let go of the world. Let me state that more emphatically: It is only from this inner place that we can shake off those things we cannot let go of in any other way.

As we experience a significant shift in our awareness, our joy is expressed as gratitude, and all we want to do is give back. Selfless service solidifies our inner shift and must become a significant aspect of our lives. Through service, we realize, "I am not the center of the universe, and life does not revolve around me." We cultivate the ability to give what is wanted, instead of what we think is needed—and this takes us beyond ourselves and beyond our desires. The capacity and willingness to serve unconditionally is one of the highest expressions of flow.

LIVING AS AN EXPRESSION OF GOD

In this chapter I have outlined some of the innumerable challenges we must work through in order to gain our freedom. So why are we willing to face all of the difficulty and the annihilation that come with seeking to know God? It can only be because we are dedicated to knowing and serving God. We trust in the design and pattern of our own Divine Life even though it is not up to us to choose how it unfolds. We simply keep weaving. There is no security and safety in spiritual growth. That can only be found in the experience of God. Ironically, all of the things we hold on to—the things we believe we need in order to live in safety and security—are exactly what keep us separate from God.

It is the living of spirituality that is important, as that is the creative gift God gave to Himself. If the Absolute One created diversity in order to experience Himself, then each one of us represents part of that diversity, and we experience God by finding Divinity in ourselves. There is a knowing in us that cannot be denied when it starts to speak. Our dedication to that inner knowledge is what provides the motivation to repeatedly walk into the fire. Nobody tells us we have to do it. Nobody forces us.

In reality, however, it is not "we" who are cultivating the longing or walking back into the fire. It is God. He is doing His dance, and we are simply part of that Graceful expression. It is only we who misunderstand, thinking we are separate from God and from that Divine Force. We must get beyond our individual struggle and experience our lives as the flow and play of creation, life radiating from the heart of God. Living in this state is true freedom. The practice of *Kuṇḍalinī* Yoga is a powerful path to that liberation.

SECTION TWO

CONSCIOUS STUDENTSHIP: THE SADHANA OF TRANSFORMATION

THE FIRE
OF CONSCIOUSNESS

4

CHAPTER FOUR

The preceding chapters have offered a vision of what is possible for anyone who engages in a spiritual life. They have provided a conceptual background, reviewing the basic principles at the core of Tantric philosophy and *Kuṇḍalinī sādhana*. In addition, I've begun to talk about the transformation that happens on the path to liberation, as well as what it might be like to live as a conscious expression of the Divine.

Now the subject turns to what it really means to be a student. This section of the book is entitled "Conscious Studentship: The *Sādhana* of Transformation," and here we will discuss the significant elements of spiritual practice from this perspective. We must learn what it is to be an authentic student, in terms of our desire for and commitment to growth, and in relation to the specific techniques and practices we must use—both in meditation and in daily life. We will explore several topics in depth, and see how they all fit together as integrated parts of our spiritual work.

The first thing we must do as students is to ask ourselves:

Where do I live? What do I focus on?

The answers to those questions reveal our response to the next, most critical inquiry: *What is it that I want in my life?* We must come to the fundamental understanding that where we live in ourselves, and what we focus on in our awareness, *is* what we want in our lives.

An honest examination of our inner state will provide the answers to the first two questions. It is not a matter of what we say is important to us but of how we use our energy. And perhaps more importantly, it is not what we think *will* be important if we can only adjust and get past some situation in our lives.

We need to distinguish between what is important to us and what happens to us, because they are separate issues. Where we live and what we focus on have nothing to do with the circumstances of our lives. Our inner state is the resonance from which we function—and the expression of that resonance is what creates our reality and our experience, no matter what is happening on the surface of daily life.

TRANSFORMING OUR CONSCIOUSNESS

It is because Divine Consciousness is always present, always within us, that we have the power to choose what is important. Consciousness is the field on which all of life manifests and expresses itself, and it has two primary aspects. First, it is the field on and from which all of life is created. It is both the Source and the form of all life. Consciousness also has the ability to know Itself. Because those two dynamics are happening in our own awareness, we can fulfill the purpose of spiritual practice, which is to transform our consciousness. It is through our conscious choice that we commit to doing the work that is necessary in order to transform our experience from one of living in duality to living in Unity, from living separate from God to living in God.

Transformation of our consciousness is exactly that. We must bring to our spiritual practice the unwillingness to accept that our limited consciousness (and therefore our limited experience in life) is all there is. To discover some deeper truth and reality, we must let go of everything in life that has reinforced, that has in fact proved to us, that we are separate from our own Source. Meditation is the way that we tune in to a completely different place, which exposes us to a deeper state of understanding and experience.

Inherent in this transformation is the recognition that we have the freedom to live wherever we want, and this means where we function from within ourselves. Absolutely none of the conditions of our lives need to change in order for us to have the conscious awareness we seek. Where we live and what we focus on is what gives us our experience of life. We either go through our day consciously creating that life, or unconsciously allowing life to create our own experience. That is why we first determine for ourselves what we really want, and then we do the work to actualize it.

OUR INNER STATE AFFECTS OUR EXPERIENCE

In order to illustrate the mechanics of how we create our life, I have created a series of five diagrams. Diagram 1 contains three circles, which describe how our experiences are limited when we are not residing in the deepest part of ourselves.

The innermost circle represents where we live inside. The second circle shows our inner state of awareness and how it radiates outward, creating a filter through which we perceive everything. If we are far from our center, the vibration or resonance that emerges from us will be what is expressed outwardly. Duality then begins to solidify, becoming our experience, our consciousness. The outer ring demonstrates that our inner state functions as a filter for processing experience, and it also serves as a means of expressing ourselves in our actions, words, thoughts, and feelings. From both these perspectives, our limited inner state ends up restricting every aspect of our lives.

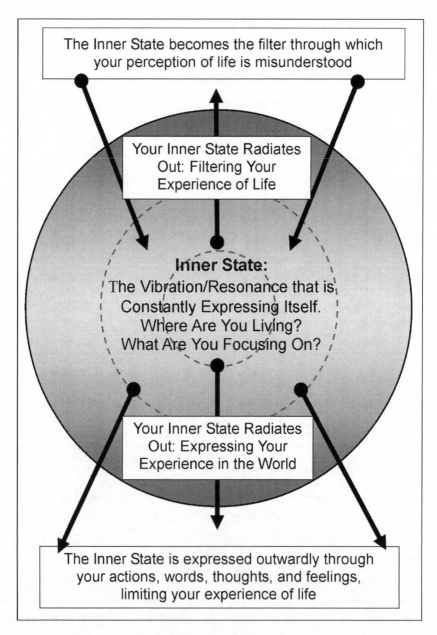

The Inner State becomes the filter through which your perception of life is misunderstood

Your Inner State Radiates Out: Filtering Your Experience of Life

Inner State:
The Vibration/Resonance that is Constantly Expressing Itself.
Where Are You Living?
What Are You Focusing On?

Your Inner State Radiates Out: Expressing Your Experience in the World

The Inner State is expressed outwardly through your actions, words, thoughts, and feelings, limiting your experience of life

Diagram 1

Our reaction to our lives is not what we must focus on—but rather the inner resonance we are reacting *from*. Our resonance is the place where we live, and it acts like a magnifying glass, highlighting and intensifying where we choose to invest our energy. It is where and what we are attuned to, a state that radiates out and influences our experience. Everything coming into us percolates through that vibration, and no matter what is happening outside us, this inner resonance creates our experience. It is never that somebody else is doing something to us, or that some event is negatively affecting us. If we function from a place of limited consciousness and misunderstanding, our interaction with life will simply reflect this restriction.

If, for example, our resonance is one of fear—if that is what we are projecting outward—our fear attracts situations that reinforce and validate this emotion. Everything is tainted by fear, and then what happens to how we express ourselves? We impose our fear on the people around us through our thoughts, emotions, projections, and so forth. Fear, worry, or insecurity is putting our attention on what we do not want to have happen. If that is our state, how could we express anything different? Our experience is immediately limited; we can't feel the love or openness around us because the environment has been bombarded with the emotions we are projecting. The critical factor is the state that radiates out. What is being projected through our thoughts and feelings—fear and hate, or love, devotion, offering, and giving? Because our inner resonance creates our reality, if we are constantly projecting tension, blame, doubt, etc., then that is going to be our experience.

THE NEED TO LIVE IN OUR CENTER

We have to be very conscious. Instead of getting caught up in what we think and feel about what is happening to us, we have to center inside ourselves and be aware of our resonance. By doing this, we accept the responsibility and recognize that what is going on has everything to do with our inner state. We understand that in order to change our experience of life, we have to change our state, and this is where we focus our attention. In other words, in order to move through the progression of transforming our limited consciousness into Divine Presence, life does not have to change. That which is limited will always be limited. But the opposite is also true—that which is infinitely open always has and always will exist, and it is always available for us to experience as our Self. It is never not open and it is never not infinite. What we are trying to do is redirect our vision from looking at what is limited to what is not.

People may feel they are restricted by their karma, but karma is not what happens to us. It is primarily how situations affect us—how far we are pulled from our center. When we transform our experience, the dynamics of our lives may not, in fact, change. Everyone wants to be free of their karma so they can have the perfect life: they want to be rich, famous, gorgeous, and, of course, enlightened. But karma is just the repetition of energy in a pattern. It is not a matter of stopping something, but of stopping the energy from repeating itself. When we get quieter, more astute, and more conscious, we begin to see our karma coming from a million miles away, and we are able to do the Michael Jackson moonwalk and sidestep its impact.

It's relatively easy to say we want to transform the place we live in, that we want to live in God's heart. The work is the application and focusing of our consciousness on what we say we want. Often we allow something else to dominate our awareness and distract or pull us away from a commitment to what we said was the most important thing in life. We must be conscious, using our capacity for self-referential awareness. We must remain cognizant of our state and not wait until we are completely out of our center before we tune back inside.

We have the control and the power to transform ourselves because God gave it to us. If we don't choose freedom now, why do we think we will choose it later, when we are potentially even more deeply mired in our patterns? For most people, life is the accumulation of more tension and karma, which takes even more effort to dissolve. Our choices of where we live, moment by moment, add up to the experience of our life. We cannot be closed, tense, and fearful day after day, year after year, and then expect a different experience as the sum of our life. We are always so surprised. We get angry and say, "Look what life did to me." Life does nothing to us. We create our own reality, even in an extreme situation where we are physically imprisoned. This does not mean that what happens to us is easy or fair—but that we have the power to decide where we are going to live, despite whatever amount of energy or type of obstacle we have to face.

Thinking that someone else is doing something to us, or that life did not work out as we wished, only reinforces our dualistic experience. It reinforces the grip of the ego and the veils of duality. What do we have to do when we recognize that our inner state is the filter that creates our experience of life? Refine the filter. We must be free of the part of us that will never, ever, understand what duality is, because it is caught in it. It doesn't make a difference what our current state is. What matters is whether we accept it as the state we are going to live in. How we got there, what plane or train took us there, is not relevant. What is pertinent is whether we are consciously aware of that state, and whether we choose to stay there or to change it.

LIFE IS TRANSFORMED WHEN WE LIVE IN OUR CENTER

When we look at Diagram 2, we see the difference created in our lives when we are living in the center of our heart. The innermost and middle circles are the same as in the first diagram, but the critical difference is that we are expressing openness and joy instead of constriction and limitation. Because of this, the outer ring has been transformed.

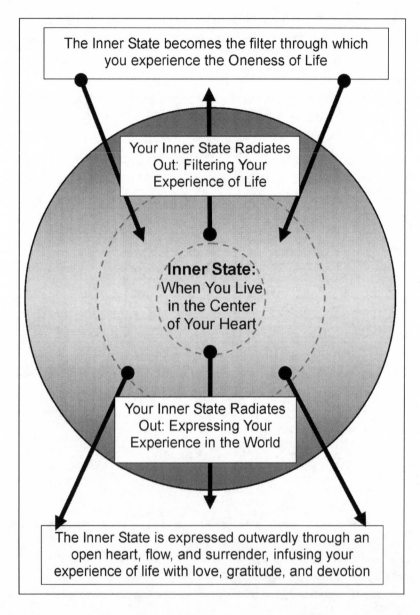

Diagram 2

Our inner state is now the resonance through which we experience the Oneness of life, and we project outward from an open heart filled with flow and surrender. This infuses life with love, gratitude, and devotion, and we have the capacity to transform our lives in every dimension. Whatever limitation we find ourselves in, whatever state we find ourselves in, no matter how dense it is or how much of a grip it has on us, our discipline is to consciously rise above it.

You could say that the way we transform our life is through fire—the fire of consciousness. As we gain the ability to burn through any density, we learn from personal experience that our outward circumstances do not have to change in order for us to live in unconditional joy.

When we pray, we usually ask to have some situation changed, so that we feel less pressured. Instead of wanting something to change, we should ask God for an internal transformation. Then, automatically, everything will change. The form may not be different, but our experience of it will change, because we have grown inside. Our vibration, resonance, and how we interpret that which radiates out and that which comes into our lives is profoundly different. We can now comprehend that sometimes the very things we pray to change are precisely those things we must meet and transform in order to gain our freedom.

The things in our life that require us to change are there because they are projected from the screen of our own consciousness, to give us something to look at and say, "I have got to grow." If we constantly want externals to change, we may get that wish, but nothing will have changed inside us. Which do you want? It is dualistic misunderstanding to think that we should, could, or would need to adjust life in order to shift our experience of it.

These diagrams are a tool to illustrate that it is vital to choose where we put our attention because that completely determines the quality of our experience. There is nothing wrong with our thoughts and feelings—except they mostly make us miserable! Thoughts, emotions, and feelings are consciousness in a limited condition. They are not separate from consciousness, but we can understand how far from infinite openness those thoughts and feelings are, and recognize that we do not have to choose to stay in this resonance. Transformation of our awareness means refining our capacity to tune in to finer vibrations of consciousness. Wherever we live is the center of our universe. Everything we say and do is created from that place, and everything we perceive is based on it as well.

TUNING IN TO A DIFFERENT RESONANCE WITHIN

There are very rare people who can recognize this reality and then find themselves immediately transformed by that knowledge. The rest of us have work to do. We penetrate through our surface density, and we reach inside, focusing our consciousness inward, back to our Source. We do this again and again, allowing ourselves to be absorbed into a finer resonance of awareness. Within every dimension of consciousness there is a deeper truth. The truth we find in the world is real, and the truth we experience as we move inside ourselves is radically different from that. One level does not negate the other. We have bodies. We can do things to them and they can die. There is truth in this physical reality—but the part of us from which the body came never dies, and those two different truths are not in conflict. We can always choose to focus our awareness in a deeper dimension. What a powerful shift, to understand that instead of constantly defending our thoughts and emotions as the only reality, we can penetrate into and live from whatever dimension we choose.

What happens when we are listening to a song about lost love? We are attuning to a resonance, which affects our mood. Like that, our state creates a field in which we play, over and over again. Everything we perceive comes through this resonance, and everything we express out of this state is informed and created by it. Because of this, we are limited to a certain vein of experience, which may be fine while it lasts, but it does not allow us to expand our capacity to contact a broader spectrum of consciousness.

There is never anything bad, or wrong, with anything. There is only a limiting effect on our consciousness and therefore on our experience of life. A spiritual life requires the conscious choice to live in what is not limited—so when we find ourselves caught in a particular frequency, we change the channel. We tune in to whatever vibration we wish to find. We might encounter heavy feelings or heavy metal in the course of adjusting our inner dial, but when we realize that wherever we stay will create the resonance we live in, we are careful to continually search for the highest vibration.

It is a matter of focusing our consciousness, being very clear about where we want to go, and not allowing our attention to get trapped in whatever vibration comes up. Sometimes when we meditate, when we try to go deeper inside, what we look for does not automatically pop up. What keeps us looking and penetrating through the density? Devotion, and focusing on the will to grow. Grace is the highest consciousness within us, and It is seeking Itself. It knows what we are looking for, because It is always in that state. That part of us is never *not* there—but whether we experience that reality is, again, a matter of where we live and what we focus on. Ultimately, it is a matter of what it is that we want.

GETTING BEYOND OUR PERSONAL DRAMA

Our feelings, emotions, and drama—no matter how good or bad they feel—are all just waves on the ocean. If we want to go scuba diving, we don't bring a surfboard. Thoughts and feelings are limiting because they don't allow us to dive beneath the surface and find an expanded consciousness. Every band of consciousness essentially has an obscuring layer on its top and bottom, and it requires concentration to penetrate through these barriers. It also requires our understanding, from a deeper place in ourselves, that the particular band we find ourselves frolicking in is not the highest experience possible.

We have this incredible need to defend our right to have thoughts and feelings. We continue to spend our time there, and this obsession boils down to the fact that we are attached to our right to be miserable. We think we won't be alive without our feelings. But what happens when we are in the grip of some emotion is that one limiting thought leads to another—this one is validating that one, and the next is validating the previous two. Soon we have forgotten what we were originally sad about and are thinking about something that has no connection to it at all. It's all an illusion, and there's nothing really to be attached to. People say, "Well, I have to go through my personal process." Where is that written? Another line is, "I have to speak my truth." Why don't we allow God to speak His truth to us?

We never defend our right to be happy, only our right to be unhappy. Love, gratitude, and devotion are emotions. Why not focus on our right to have *those* feelings? If we spent as much energy insisting on our right to be happy, instead of our right to be unhappy, what an amazing difference there would be in our resonance.

When people are grumpy or get fixated on something they usually don't take advice very well. Everything happens within the spectrum of our ego, and it's important not to underestimate the power it has to protect itself as a separate entity. The ego is inherently limited in its consciousness and in its capacity to experience or understand anything other than itself. We are trapped within that limited perspective, which is why it is so difficult to get past the grip of the ego without some help.

From within that limited perspective we only make limited choices about where we focus and where we live. This is why we need a teacher—someone who can remind us that we are always choosing the state from which we function. The whole purpose of spiritual practice is to break out of that bind and open to the infinite possibilities for experience within.

THE PROGRESSION TOWARD FREEDOM

In the process of transforming our consciousness from perceiving duality to living in Unity, we move through three basic stages. First, we must free ourselves from the grip of the ego—from that part of us that believes and acts as if it is separate from God. This means moving past being caught up in all the dynamics and drama of life, which is the camouflage the ego throws up to mask its true nature. We free ourselves from being at the mercy of the ups and downs of daily life by recognizing and transcending all of our tensions and patterns. In essence, we are opening to a deeper place within, internalizing our energy, and moving beyond the ego's limited perception.

Having passed that initial stage, we gain the capacity to see the deeper ways the ego binds us. These are the subtle veils of duality, which reinforce our perceived separation. They create the experience that we are separate, that we are different, and that we are the doer. It is only when we have worked through the ego's smoke screen of drama and tension that we are able to deal with these subtler barriers to liberation.

As we finally dissolve these veils, we can move into the center of God's heart, becoming a conscious living expression of the Divine. All of life is that living expression, but the vital transformation is having the conscious awareness of that Grace. In this state we have dissolved all duality and simply experience the unity of all life as Divine Presence—that consciousness which is always present, always within us.

Every day we choose to live wherever we want. Instead of remaining in a limited state we can choose to move toward our center and experience our highest Self. This happens through the conscious process of continually reaching back inside. Diagram 3 illustrates how that progression is one of freeing ourselves from the grip of the ego, dissolving the veils of duality, and becoming a conscious living expression of the Divine. The outer circle shows the ego's grip on us, the middle circle represents the veils of duality, and the inner circle is the freedom of living as the Divine.

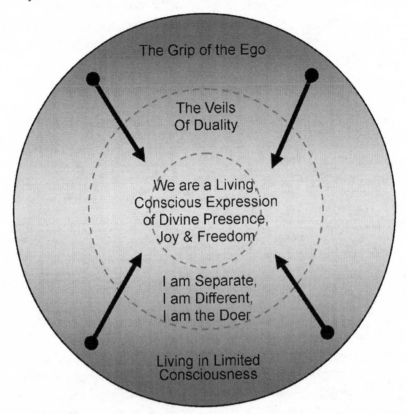

Diagram 3

Through this transformation we are eventually able to dissolve the misunderstanding that we are separate from God. When we experience that we are not separate or different, we also realize that we are therefore not the agent. We are not the doer but simply a dancer on the field of life.

It is imperative that we free ourselves from the grip and action of the ego. That is the only way to break through our surface tensions and get to the true Source of our separation and suffering. Then we can consciously transform and dissolve the veils of duality in order to merge into our Source. The grip of the ego functions like the waves on the ocean, the waves crashing against the beach. There are multitudes of them and they have every kind of form.

What is incredible about the ocean is that we only see the surface when looking at the waves. But of course there are tremendous currents that move around the ocean floor, which are miles deep and miles wide. As they travel very slowly around the planet, these currents dictate and create the field of the ocean, which in turn affects the surface, including the waves.

Like the deeper ocean currents, the veils of duality contain our continuing patterns—and therefore so much of the surface activity we engage in is not what we think it is. These powerful undercurrents and patterns within us are not only creating the field on which our actions are performed, but are also the reason we act as we do. In addition, the veils mask the true power and source of the ocean of Consciousness. It is therefore only when we penetrate through the veils of duality to the innermost circle that our life transcends all limitations and we become simply an expression of Divine Consciousness. As we move outward from the center, the veils hide and confuse everything.

It's important to understand that we must use our awareness in two ways if we wish to grow. First, we need to be responsible for the manifestation of life—those waves on the beach—because we might need to modify some aspects of our outer behavior. But in addition to that, we have to penetrate through the surface noise and begin to really understand the source of the pain, difficulty, and confusion that causes all of this action that is performed within the grip of the ego. We have to face the deeper pain of separation from God.

Central to living as a conscious expression of the Divine is the experience and understanding that we are the ocean of Consciousness. How amazing that a single individuated drop in the vastness of water can somehow believe it is separate! We are in the middle of the ocean, five miles deep. There is nothing in sight, and yet we are somehow convinced we are different from that which surrounds us.

When we think we are separate and different, duality is established, and we suffer. How could it ever be possible for there to be a wave without the ocean? The wave is simply the energy of the ocean, the energy of this incredible depth that breathes and pulsates.

The progression toward liberation therefore requires a major transformation within us. We are still the same drop of water, playing in the waves. And the ocean, with its various forms and currents, is still the ocean. What changes is our understanding and our consciousness. It is a transformation of what we are conscious of, and what we allow to be the limits of that consciousness. Even the most superficial action of the ego is not separate from the Divine Consciousness that gives it life, or from the Divine Energy that gives it the power to express that life. We only experience it as something separate, and we then seek to prove that this perspective is true. This is the defense of the ego, trying to maintain the position of "I am separate; I am the doer." This is the drama we engage in, day after day, month after month, year after year, decade after decade, lifetime after lifetime. That energy goes around in horizontal circles, keeping us on the surface of life. Our attention is caught in these self-reinforcing loops, and we cannot go deeper without consciously breaking the grip of the ego.

MOVING BEYOND WHAT GRABS OUR ATTENTION

Diagram 4 was designed to help clarify how our inner freedom is obscured by the veils of duality and masked by the grip of the ego. It shows how we continually re-create our dualistic experience. This is the dimension within ourselves from which our patterns of self-absorption and karma solidify into the strongest binding and the deepest level of dualistic misunderstanding. The outer circle represents the grip of the ego, where we live in limited consciousness. What we see in this outer ring are the actions that spring from this density of consciousness.

The Grip of the Ego

Perceptions   Contractions

Caught in   The Veils
Condition   Of Duality   Projections

Resistance   Emotions

Drama   When Our Divine
          State is Obscured   Doubt
          We Experience
Desires   Duality   Lust

          I am Separate,
Attachments   I am Different,   Tensions
          I am the Doer

Thought-   Need to
Constructs   Control

Limited Consciousness

Diagram 4

The constant activity and motion on this level are very real, and we are absorbed by these waves on the surface of our life. Our engagement here completely consumes our awareness, and for most people, this is the primary flavor of their experience. The dominant force may perhaps be the need to control or the projection of fear, but the common denominator is that the ego is busily generating all of this projection, all of this mental and emotional turmoil. Because we are so dominated by the ego, we cannot see ourselves clearly. We cannot see that there is a different experience available to us.

If we truly want to be free and live in the highest consciousness within, we must transcend the grip of the ego and move past our internal struggle. This means becoming more than the part of us that creates all this diverse activity to grab our attention, to fool us into thinking that this is the full range of life. We struggle and fight with ourselves, over and over again. The noise level of our drama can be numbing, and so we must again ask ourselves these critical questions: Where has my attention been? What is my focus? Where do I live? What is the endless struggle that I find myself engaged in?

The place we each get stuck can probably be identified by one of the words in the outer circle of the diagram. It may feel like this is all life consists of—and if we are trapped in these surface thoughts and emotions, our experience is, in fact, very limited. However, this entire dimension is just an effect of the deeper pain and suffering we experience every moment of our lives.

When we are not willing, strong, and courageous enough to face the ultimate pain of separation, we create our own waves of surface unrest. So as we move in toward the center of the diagram, what we see is simply that the experience of duality, of separateness, is the source of our pain and suffering. No amount of sporting in the waves in the grip of the ego will change that.

Just as our clothes are an outer covering, 99 percent of our actions do not really touch on the critical issue of our lives. They are the effect of our deeper misunderstanding. What we do is mask that misunderstanding because it is too painful to address it. It is painful to recognize, and it is painful to move past it. This is why it requires incredible intensity to burn through our limitations and to transform ourselves. I have described the veils of duality as the belief that "I am separate, I am different, and I am the doer," and this is always the underlying theme of our personal drama. In our own movie the names, places, and characters change, but our experience does not really change, because we have not changed where we function from.

EXPOSING OUR DEEPER ISSUES

When we dig inside those veils, we begin to expose, confront, and hopefully dissolve our ingrained patterns of self-hate, self-rejection, and self-absorption. This is what manifests as the characteristics displayed in the outer circle of the diagram. The patterns wrapped inside the veils are the most powerful means of reinforcing our separation, and they are what we are working to change.

If, for example, we are caught in the need to control, we can track that back inside. What would really be the source of the need to control? Fear of death? Trace this back to an even deeper level and we encounter the belief that we are separate—and therefore when we die, we will just dissolve into dust.

We must have the conscious discrimination to look and see what is truly reinforcing the misunderstanding that we are separate. It is not something superficial like our fear of commitment in relationships. That is just a wave crashing on the beach. When we are aware of that level of action and consciously begin to transform it, the underlying pattern is exposed. Note, however, that if we don't transform the action, the patterns will never be exposed. If, for example, we are anxious, we may take a pill and feel better, but what have we really done? We have used our unconsciousness to avoid something, instead of becoming conscious and locating the source of our anxiety. Spiritual inquiry is always a process of consciously looking deeper within and uncovering whatever is masking reality or reinforcing our misunderstanding.

We have to free the energy and the awareness within the limited consciousness of the ego's tenacious grip. We do this by transcending it, burning it, and transforming it from a level of density into one of energy, and love. The freeing of these blocks creates an inner flow of energy that can penetrate deeper into us. We deal with it not by fighting and struggling but by understanding that what we should be doing is recognizing the Divine Consciousness underneath the surface.

An authentic spiritual person is prepared to uncover and dissolve whatever is an obstacle to realization. When we are centered in Unity, all diverse action is an expression of that state. As soon as we move away from Unity, there is "me" and "not me," and this dichotomy leads us to engage in the continual re-creation of a dualistic experience.

From the highest perspective, diversity is part of the expression of Oneness, but within the veil of duality we don't know that. We are afraid to give up our identity, to completely merge into Divine Presence—because then we won't be here to identify! The result is that we stay trapped in duality.

Burning Through Our Deepest Obstacles

The patterns, the karma, and the truly profound trauma that we experience and carry with us are the glue and the substance of the veils of duality. This is what we must dissolve. To discover the buried treasure of Unity, we have to burn through the layers of unconsciousness, which tend to get denser and denser as we continue to repeat the same patterns.

Lifetime after lifetime, we have not faced our basic misunderstanding that we are separate from God—and perhaps the deepest pattern is one of avoiding the very things we must open to in order to free ourselves. When we get too close to whatever we would rather not recognize about ourselves, the first thing we do is buy a ticket to go on vacation, or engage in denial or attack. Instead of burning through our obstacles, we remain in the outer circle where our projections, fears, and resistance dominate. We miss the perfect opportunity to free ourselves from what truly binds us and keeps us separate.

Even when we have reached a very deep place inside, there are still hidden crevices of misunderstanding and ego—and if we are lucky, they will be exposed and become apparent. Those are precisely the patterns that will keep us bound if we do not expose them. And often, even it they are revealed, we don't accept the insight into what needs to be changed in ourselves. We avoid coming to terms with ourselves by saying things like, "I am too spiritual for this . . . this is not my fault . . . this is someone else's fault."

The only solution to the difficulties we face in our spiritual growth is to open, and be conscious. Be aware of these deep states from which life is expressing itself. Know what you want and don't stop until you see the white of God's eyes. We must know what we want, and then we must not forget it when the potential realization is masked by some level of duality, by some veil. The stronger our wish, the deeper we penetrate into ourselves, the stronger the ego's reaction will be, creating a seducing scene to grab our attention and divert us.

This defensive power of the ego is like one of those really thin plastic membranes. One can press almost through it and then it throws you back out. Like that, if we are not paying close attention, we land far away from the change we were trying to effect.

FINDING OPENNESS AND CONSCIOUSNESS IN OURSELVES

Let's look at Diagram 5. What is different about this picture? Diagram 5 represents a state of openness and consciousness, the opposite of Diagram 4. When we are closed and unconscious, we learn how to open and become conscious in order to transform negative thoughts and emotions into their opposite qualities. When we feel we are projecting, we pull back and go inside, not allowing that energy to manifest. Our work is to stay centered in our highest Self and engage life from there—to be conscious and aware of ourselves. We are always expressing our state, whether we are trapped in duality or established in Unity with God.

Diagram 5

Consciousness is the field on which our life is projected, and we are never separate from our awareness. We have to find that place inside and express it in our experience. In other words, we have to create our experience by what we find in ourselves. I cannot overemphasize the importance of deep meditation on a regular basis—to make contact with a higher consciousness and make it our own, so we can use it to transform our experience. If we do not transform ourselves in every moment, in every dynamic of life, we should not be surprised if we never in our lifetime cut through the crust of the ego. It is just too thick to dissolve unless we regularly open to a completely different dimension inside.

In our search for God, all duality must be dissolved. Whether we get caught in some minutia or come face-to-face with profound patterns in ourselves, we work to transcend our boundaries. Divine Energy is always present, always within us, and it is our gift to use it for its intended purpose of freeing ourselves. Liberation is the abolishing of any fragrance of separation. Anything less is a sad reward for all of our hard work. When one is free, there is no longer a "you" debating with yourself about whether or not you are separate or still in the grip of the ego. You are simply a living expression of the Divine.

THE WISH TO GROW

5

CHAPTER FIVE

The magnificent power that creates the infinite expansion of the universe exists within us, and manifests in our lives as the wish to grow. Rudi often said, "The wish to grow is the most powerful force within a human being." We focus on the simplicity of our wish, on the sweet desire to know that God dwells within us as our Self. Our spiritual work is to consciously deepen our wish and, equally important, to always keep it in sight. The capacity to tune back in to our wish when we have lost it and can't connect to it is the true test of that wish and the true fortification of it within us. We are all either consciously choosing to grow or we are unconsciously choosing not to grow. Growing spiritually only happens through our conscious wish, effort, and Grace.

Most of us require a lifetime of cultivating our wish and committing to a spiritual practice in order to unfold enough inner depth to completely transform our consciousness. It's so easy to say we want to grow and then not do the work necessary to create real openness inside, or make decisions from a place that truly wants to grow. If growing spiritually is not the most important thing for us, we will not attain the freedom and the immersion into God that we say we want. It is a lot of work—but it is a joyous work if approached with a profound sense of gratitude for the opportunity to grow.

THE WISH CAN PENETRATE THROUGH ANY DENSITY

My teacher Rudi was a person who worked intensely. By his own admission, he lived under enormous pressure and tension, and had to overcome tremendous thickness in himself. Yet he never ever let that get in the way of opening his heart deeper. He was a New York Jew who grew up in the Depression and expressed himself in a very direct way. Rudi would always say, "Any schmuck can do it when it is easy."

Rudi spoke often of times when he would literally sit for eight hours straight and repeat to himself, "I wish to grow." As that mantra penetrated within him, he went through an extraordinary range of experiences, from hysteria to total stillness. Sometimes there was such complete resistance that he wanted to get up and run away. Despite everything, Rudi would continue to drill inside in his effort to contact an ever-deepening level of "I wish to know myself."

The wonderfully frightening news about the power of this wish is that it will work. We are reaching inside, asking the God who dwells within to show Himself to us. Then, when God takes us seriously, we must stand back and let that power do whatever is necessary to change us. *Kuṇḍalinī sādhana* is often described as the practice of fire, of transformation by fire.

Asking to know our own Self releases incredible energy within us, and this enables the process to give us the very thing we asked for. However, it is not up to us to determine exactly what that process will require of us or what our life will look like. When change starts to happen we can't say, "I meant, I wish to grow because . . . or only if . . . or when." There is a reason we put a period at the end of "I wish to grow." Our wish must be unconditional.

It is important that on a regular basis—daily, if possible—we get in contact with our wish to grow. We go back to the clarity of our intention and get in contact with it, energizing and reinforcing it within ourselves so that there is never a moment when our wish is not available to us as the transforming agent of our experience. In every moment and in every dimension of life, we can choose the experience we are having. Even when circumstances and conditions grab and squeeze us, creating a feeling that there is nothing inside, we can still have openness simply by wishing it to be so. This is the power of our wish.

ACTIVATING AN INNER FORCE

According to Tantric philosophy, it is Śiva's wish, Śiva's will, that gives rise to all of life, including us as individuated expressions of Him. Through our own will and wish, we, in turn, create the experience of our life. So we have to ask, "What is the experience I am creating for myself?" From within ourselves we project a set of circumstances, a dance we can either learn well, or stumble and bumble through. We can get caught up in the confusion, mistakenly viewing the dynamic as something separate from us, or we can recognize that life always presents us with the perfect situation through which we can find unlimited freedom.

The powerful, all-knowing capacity within us continually creates dynamics in our lives that test our ability to expand our center and grow. We must use every opportunity to work inside, instead of trying to rewrite what is happening in the external dimension.

The experience we are having in our life is a reflection of the place we make contact with inside. We use our wish to drill through more superficial levels of contact, and to continue focusing within until we meet a place of complete clarity. This is the power of the wish and the simplicity of that power. Yet our wish, like everything in life, is an expression of consciousness. When we come in contact with a spiritual force, it is by asking deeply and connecting to the wish in us that allows the force to do the work of transforming us. Our job is to get out of the way of this transformation.

The trick is to survive our wish. Just the simple act of saying, "I wish to grow" will activate an energy that will push all your buttons. Tremendous resistance will surface—more than you could ever imagine was possible within yourself. Of course, there is the old cliché, "Be careful what you wish for." When we desire to know the God within, we are asking for no less than the annihilation of the part of us that doesn't know it is Divine. So in that process of profound transformation, we must experience both expansion and dissolution—the expansion of the Divinity within us, and the dissolution of the boundary of our limited self.

DECIDING WHAT WE REALLY WANT

It is not really relevant whether this transformation is difficult or not. What is relevant is that if we decide we really want to know God, we must make our own spiritual freedom the most important thing to us, and not let living get in the way of that focus. We all know that if we allow life to get in the way, it will. This is not to reject life, but to understand that it requires a big investment of time and energy to really go inside and permanently live in our heart. There is an element of sacrifice in our wish and our effort to grow spiritually. If we are expending ourselves elsewhere, we may not have enough resources left to do our spiritual work. Each of us has to decide if we have the capacity to make liberation our highest priority, because if it is, we must be prepared to make some trade-offs.

Maintaining an inner focus is a struggle only if we allow it to be. We are usually conflicted because we have something in our lives that we do not want—or else we don't have whatever we think we need! There is nothing wrong with wanting anything. However, it is most important to deeply accept what we do have and to understand that we actually have within ourselves so much that we are not in contact with. This is the real treasure, which makes all the surrender and all the hard work worthwhile.

One of the fundamental mistakes people make is to give so much meaning to what we endure on a daily basis. This level of activity is just the rent we pay for being on earth. We give meaning to everything when we are established in our hearts, and act from that place. Then no matter what we are doing, there is no difference in our experience.

Spiritual work is profoundly simple, yet we make it seem so complicated. We sit and meditate to get in tune with the resonance of the Divine within. We bring up a deeper reservoir of energy and awareness, and then we carry that resonance into our life. This is not retreating from the world but engaging the world from our center. We call this "work" because there is a constant consciousness of reaching back to connect, regardless of what we are doing. Within us is the capacity to feel our hearts and to feel the flow every second of the day. When we talk about reaching a permanent state of awareness, a permanent state of surrender, it means we are immersed in that consciousness. That is our life. There is no distinction between the inner and the outer, and that is the ultimate realization.

Focusing on a Place of Openness

Sometimes our day is about finding our heart and simply being able to feel something. Other days we are tuned in to the flow or are even in the state of Presence. In each stage of our growth we focus on different things. Ideally, we could simply hear, "God is One, without a second," and nothing else would need to be said or done in order for us to have the experience of that reality. However, that is not the level of consciousness we bring to our lives. When something inside us says it is time to wake up and we come to our spiritual practice, that voice is God's Grace. The rest is our work—the work we need to do to attain our liberation—

and we begin by continually bringing our attention inside and cultivating our wish to grow.

Every day we have to make a conscious effort and make conscious choices. When we forget, we refocus. The fact that we remember again is wonderful. Instead of shoving energy against a contraction, we find our wish and project our energy back inside. All of a sudden, there is openness in us and we no longer feel tight. When we meditate, we get quiet, feel our heart open, and then begin to work from a simple place of openness. When we open our eyes, we engage and consume life from that place, instead of being consumed by life. This state is foundational. If you accomplish nothing in your day, or in your life, except to find that state of openness, then choose to do that. We must bring joy and gratitude to every aspect of life, including the challenges. They are what can potentially really nourish us and are the test of what we say is important in our lives.

ACCEPTING RESPONSIBILITY FOR OURSELVES

It is our mind and emotions that keep us from remembering, that take us out of our center. We always want to blame our inattention on somebody else's brain or somebody else's emotion. Where we live from is our choice. Where somebody else lives from is their choice. Just because the world around us functions from some other place, and dealing with people and circumstances is often hard, this does not mean we have to lose our center.

Unfortunately, other people have a powerful capacity to inflict their tensions on us. We do not have to take on that tension, but we do have to be very quiet and aware because what they're saying may be feedback critical to our understanding of the changes we need to make in ourselves. That is different than allowing anybody, ever, to take us out of our center. If we are quiet and centered, it tends to threaten everyone around us. People are going to do things to try to disrupt our harmony, because they do not experience it, and they are not comfortable around it. We have a choice every minute of the day. What are we going to choose? We should never look back and blame somebody else for the fact that we were taken out of ourselves. It is never their fault, regardless of how badly we are treated or how weird or difficult the situation is.

If something or someone hurts our heart, all too often we close it and say, "I'm never going to open again." Well, who suffers in that case? Not the person who did something to you twenty years ago. He is long gone and may not even remember you by now. This is not to deny the existence of what happened, but to understand that we can always find a deeper place within—and ultimately a place that has no conditions and is not affected by whatever happened. That is realization.

If we wish to experience the ever-present Divine force within, we must start every day with a simple act of consciousness—of getting in contact with ourselves, opening our heart, creating a flow, and carrying that awareness throughout our day.

It has been said that happiness is not the goal. Happiness is the path. If we choose to be miserable every day, how can we think that realization will simply manifest at some later date? We must think very carefully about what we truly want in our life and about what will be meaningful throughout life and at the end of life. Then we must choose it and not let anything get in the way of actualizing our choice. We are the only force that can undercut our own priorities. Choose to be happy and do your inner work, and then understand that at certain times, this will take effort.

The challenges and crises we encounter are really blessings because they have the potential to wake us up. Most people run away from difficulties, but Rudi ran toward them because he knew that dealing with the tension, the challenge, and the contraction would force him to find a deeper place in himself and thereby make him a bigger person. He said, "If there's a harder way, show it to me. It must be wonderful."

If we are growing, we will go through very difficult times of change. We must change where we live from within, and the consciousness with which we respond to the challenge. If we live from our heart, then the difficulty of any situation becomes nourishment and fuel for growth. There is a great martial arts saying, "A man rises by that which he falls." It is absolutely true. We choose the direction of our life and grow from every experience. Circumstances may change, but they do not change that choice.

On some days life beats us up and other days we are flying high, but happiness has nothing to do with any condition. If we get caught in circumstances, then we are allowing ourselves to be taken out of the place that is always truly happy, no matter what the conditions are. That is why we get up every day and face the challenges of our life with an open heart.

In times of change we often try to hold on to what we think is leaving us instead of looking at the possibility of what is coming. Something may have to be taken out of us to make room for that higher, deeper energy in us to really emerge.

DEEPENING OUR COMMITMENT

From the perspective of living consciously we open to every change, even if it is hard to undergo. A person once asked Rudi, "Do you believe in heaven and hell?" In response he said, "Yeah, I believe in heaven and hell. Hell is having to live with yourself, and heaven is going to live with God." That is the choice we make every day. It's important to understand that the wish to grow and the discipline of practice must mature into commitment. The commitment is to find the ability to hold on to our wish every day, in the face of all the adversity that life offers us.

Spirituality equals depth over time. If we cannot make the commitment and hold to it, we cannot grow. There will be a few major distractions that repeat themselves over and over again, and these are what really test our commitment. Distraction can take many forms. It might be our ambition to have a lot of money, to save the world, to live a life of luxury, to have a partner, or however our particular issues manifest.

Each person faces the challenge of the patterns of their own lifetimes, as well as their repeated karmic patterns. Inevitably, something seemingly critical arises in our life—some major theme that becomes more important than our spiritual life. This is why it is vital that our wish matures into unshakable commitment.

As we reach deeper inside, we expose more entrenched levels of our own bondage, our own suffering, and our own contractions. That is how we free ourselves. Growing spiritually is not about feeling good all the time. It is about genuinely growing, and reaching depths within ourselves that are only attainable through profound mastery of some form of practice, and a good deal of effort. My advice is to find a practice that you can do from the depth of your heart, and do it from there. The Dalai Lama said it most beautifully: "There are thousands of paths to God. Choose one, do it, and become a master at it." Do whatever brings you to God. Just don't engage in so many practices that your attention is completely split between them, or you are so busy that you forget what you were trying to accomplish in the first place.

UNLOCKING THE INNER DOOR

It is our deep wish to grow coupled with a willingness to live in a state of surrender that unlocks the door inside and opens our heart. Surrender is an internal experience, a state of awareness we inhabit. There is an old saying, "If you keep doing what you have always done, you will keep getting what you have always gotten." How beautiful. If we truly want God to come into our heart we must surrender in ourselves and draw on our inner resources to keep our attention focused on growing. Living in the service of a higher force, we continually bring all our energy and focus into our heart. Our resolve is a commitment that affirms, "I *am* going to do this."

We are not who we think we are. As we work deeper, we recognize that we are not our mind and we are not our emotions. We still have them, but they are not what we truly are, nor where we want to live from. If we wish to experience a deeper reality, we must push past our boundaries, including the limitation in our mind that defines who we are, says we cannot do something, or believes it is too hard to grow. Maybe it is hard. So what? We simply have to draw from a deeper resolve and a deeper source inside. This is what provides the strength and energy to get past ourselves. We sit down and reach that place inside and then we hold on to it. In a sense once we reach that place, it is holding on to us.

When we want to develop the capacity to grow spiritually, a disciplined practice is critical. We need to go to the gym every day to build a muscle system. Sometimes we want to go and sometimes we do not, but we know that if building powerful muscles is important to us, we must have the discipline to do the work. The same principle applies to spiritual practice. We create an inner discipline so that when our resistance comes up, we fall back on the strength of and attachment to our wish, and we practice even when we do not want to.

In some ways, as we go deeper, the resistance gets worse because a deeper part of us is now facing its own dissolution. Our ego is going to put up a tremendous fight for its survival. Rudi believed that our wish to grow is tested every day by the choices we must make, moment to moment, to hold on to that wish. Growing spiritually is the hardest thing one can ever do in life. There is no way around it.

If we seek that treasure, then we hold on to our wish and our commitment no matter how difficult it is or how long it takes. We have to find a place in us that does not struggle with the process. We repeatedly throw ourselves into the fire, even if we have not yet achieved the results we thought we should have attained. Yet, through all of our struggle and sacrifice, if we think of ourselves as martyrs, we have only boxed ourselves in to another mental construct. If we are profoundly happy even in our sacrifice, then the hard work we do is not painful. It is challenging and it may be difficult, but there is a joy in it.

Many ancient scriptures say that we have one purpose in having this human life, and that is to gain our inner freedom. Going inside, facing ourselves, and having to genuinely transcend our issues is what produces real liberation. Isn't it amazing how some inner knowingness understands the true treasure of our existence? Yet, somehow, we do not put nearly as much of our energy into the pursuit of liberation as we do into chasing after worldly endeavors. It really speaks to the capacity of humans to live very superficially.

When we deeply wish to grow and have the discipline necessary to actualize that wish a significant shift takes place in us. We start out limited—not recognizing our Divinity—but ultimately are transformed into Divinity. This is a radical change that requires a deep level of commitment and surrender. It requires more than having a brief feeling of resolve or an idealistic vision. We must be committed to working, to really feeling a change inside of us.

It will take some time of regular practice before we are able to effect that change, so resolve to keep reaching inside. The shift in our awareness comes from having the experience of finding that deeper place again and again. There is only one true resolve— to become free by living in a state that is not dependent on any condition. Be resolved to live in the heart of God, and recognize that whatever we do should be in service to that intention.

The Relationship With an Authentic Teacher

6

Chapter Six

The single purpose of our lives is to understand and experience that God dwells within us as ourselves. The single purpose of having a relationship with a teacher is for support in that discovery. Working with a teacher is an integral part of *Kuṇḍalinī sādhana* because the transmission of *śaktipāta* is the means of awakening the *Kuṇḍalinī* within a student. Through *śaktipāta*, the teacher unconditionally transmits love and energy, the fire that ignites and sustains our inner growth. *Śaktipāta* carries the living spiritual force held within a lineage of teachers—a timeless thread of tradition that has its source in God.

A teacher who embodies the energy field of his or her lineage is like a tuning fork that allows us to resonate with a deeper dimension in ourselves. The transformation of our resonance is essentially how we change our consciousness. Although this higher vibration is already within each of us, we need a teacher to help us tune in to it because we haven't yet refined the inner mechanism to do this on our own. It is receiving the living energy of *śaktipāta* from the teacher that provides the catalyst for the development of our own connection to Divinity.

Why We Need a Teacher

The nature of the teacher-student relationship has been eloquently described by the Sufi poet Kabir, who says that the true friend introduces us to our inner friend. In other words, having a teacher provides access to recognizing our own Divinity—by arousing that Divinity within us and supporting us as it unfolds.

It is never that we discover anything in the teacher; it is only that we discover something in ourselves. Perhaps the definition of an authentic student is someone who not only says they want to grow but is willing to be changed in the process. The responsibility we have as students is to take deeply, and the responsibility the teacher has to us is to give deeply and unconditionally.

Any discussion about teacher-student relationships starts with the question, "Do I need a teacher?" If we look at any scriptures, from ancient to modern times, all of them state that finding our Divinity on our own is not possible—or at least, unlikely. Some traditions are adamant that it is not possible. The ancient Tantric Shaivite text The Śiva Sutras says emphatically, "The guru is the means." The term guru does not mean "bringer of light" but rather "dispeller of darkness." The light in the guru is the same as that in the student. The teacher is simply trying to help us turn it on.

Why do we want a teacher? Or, why do we accept the need to have a teacher even if we don't exactly want one? If there is nothing in a teacher that is not in the student, why do we need help to find that which is already inside us? What can a teacher do for us?

The teacher has experienced Divinity, both in himself and in his students. He has made the transition from living in duality to living in Unity, and can therefore serve as a guide for the journey ahead. Without a reliable map any traveler may waste a lot of time or even get lost. Our spiritual journey has been compared to a twenty-minute ferry ride that would take us twenty days without the guidance of an experienced ferryman. Because we do not know how to navigate the currents, we need someone to help us across, to significantly shorten the trip. The teacher serves as the ferryman who takes us from the world of the ego to the dimension of our Self. Inherent in the role of a teacher is not only providing guidance but also the energy and nourishment we need to sustain us on this journey.

LIGHTING THE FIRE OF TRANSFORMATION

In a relationship with a teacher two things happen. First there is the spark that lights the fire, and at that point we might be tempted to say, "Okay, the fire is lit; now I'll go on my way." Why do we then stay with a teacher? Because we are so busy taking blankets and trying to cover up the fire that it keeps going out. If the flame would simply burst into light and burn away all the resistance and tension that continually come up, then we wouldn't need to have a regular, steady engagement with a teacher. Unfortunately, experience proves that this does not seem to be the case. So the second thing we need from a teacher is the continued support to keep that fire alive.

A relationship with an authentic teacher is really about the transformation of our consciousness. Our Divinity is deeply buried underneath the misunderstanding and limited perspective of our ego. The arousal of that Divinity springs from Grace, which takes the form of contact with the living spiritual force in the teacher. His energy opens us to what is already present inside. Then, as our Divinity unfolds, we need the teacher's continual support to navigate the battle with the ego, which steadfastly refuses to change. We are talking about a radical transformation, from living with our ego to living in the Divine.

Therefore the right question to ask is not, "Do I need or want a teacher?" but "Do I want to be transformed? Do I have the courage to be changed?" Engaging in a relationship with a teacher is crucial, because it means we have a relationship with an energy field that provides us with nourishment. That support gives us the strength to find a deeper place in ourselves. However, it is never the teacher who is transforming the student. We have to make the effort to engage that energy field—to open to it, deeply absorb it, and allow it to feed us—so that growth can take place. Abhinavagupta says of the teacher-student relationship:

> *Ultimately, entering into a relationship with a teacher is the conscious choice on the part of the student to place his finite awareness in direct confrontation with the expanded consciousness of the teacher, which is the unbounded consciousness the student wishes to attain. This meeting of finite and infinite consciousness represents the very condition of vimarsa, consciousness doubling back on itself, the method of realization that abides perpetually in and as the Divine Heart.*

> *As the student comes into the gaze of the guru his finite consciousness encounters its own Source in the person of the teacher. It releases the inner meditative current—the liberating Grace, the self-referential nature of the unbounded consciousness of Śiva. In the process the teacher binds the student to service and growth and the inner practices required—the single purpose of the binding is the attainment of freedom. The teacher acts as God's agent, to free the student from themselves. This all happens through śaktipāta, the will of Śiva that has taken the disciple into the gaze of the guru.*

A Relationship Beyond Duality

The outcome of the teacher-student relationship is that we discover our own Divinity, and paradoxically, in that discovery we realize there is no duality—even though there appears to be a "student" and a "teacher." In spiritual practices, it is often said that when a person needs a teacher, the teacher shows up. It is not that the teacher goes looking for you. When something in us says, "I want to wake up," it presents itself to some teacher. If we trust our own Divinity and if we trust God, and God puts a teacher in front of us—then we need to think carefully about the significance of that teacher appearing in our lives.

Although the transmission of energy (*śaktipāta*) arouses something already inside each of us, we have the experience of a palpable receiving. In reality, however, there is no duality, there is no inner and outer. We feel some energy from the teacher and believe we receive it from out there, but "out there" and "in here" are just our concepts. The Divinity within us creates, from within Itself, a situation that appears as a teacher giving to a student. The Self is serving the Self. If we understand that everything in life is happening within one whole Unity, we transcend what appears to be a paradox in the teacher-student relationship.

An authentic teacher is always committed to serving unconditionally, to working in such depth that eventually there is nothing left of himself and only God remains. An authentic student is committed to serving unconditionally, to working in such depth that eventually there is nothing left of himself and only God remains. Teacher and student are both merging with the same Self, yet the teacher serves as a source of vital energy that the student can resonate with and consume. In so doing, the student can achieve the same inner mastery of the teacher and become permanently immersed in that force.

Dimensions of the Teacher-Student Relationship

There are three dimensions to the relationship with a teacher, and a student will interact with a teacher on multiple levels at the same time. The teacher is simultaneously:

- an individual with particular personality traits
- someone who functions as a guide
- a source of transmitted energy

Let's first consider our relationship with the teacher as a person. It's really challenging for many people to get past the idea that the teacher is a person, and like everyone, he has work to do. As long as a teacher embodies a human form, he can make mistakes and have limitations and weaknesses. Unfortunately, there is no way of getting around that. In having a relationship with a human teacher, we accept that this is part of the dynamic. A student cannot look for, or expect, perfection in this aspect of the teacher.

It is incredibly easy to get caught up in the personal dimension and say, "I am not listening to this; it's just that limited, weak person who is asking me to do something." This kind of thinking presents us with a very tricky situation because even if the teacher appears imperfect in some ways, the student's ego fundamentally does not want to change—and it's very easy to project a shortcoming on the teacher as an excuse to avoid the kind of profound transformation that is required to grow spiritually.

The essence of all interaction between student and teacher is transmission. That's why it is really not important whether or not we like him, or whether we take everything he says as gospel. Inherent in verbal communication is the opportunity for the listener to define and analyze what he is hearing rather than take the speech in as energy. The primary things I encourage a student to do are establish a connection with the energy, follow it back to its Source, and take in the nourishment that is being offered. The energy in a teacher is not his alone but rather a force that flows though him. The physical teacher is never the limitation.

The Teacher's Function as a Guide

The second aspect of the teacher is something we can call the "function." Although we have to separate the function from the person of the teacher, they are integrally related. We are still dealing with the interchange between the teacher and student as two individuals. However, the function of the teacher is guidance, which emerges from a dimension within a teacher that is beyond his limited perspective. As a teacher, offering guidance is part of the responsibility that I accept. It is a challenging task, because students often don't ask for guidance—or even if they do, they are not really willing to receive and act on it.

The function of the teacher is to help his students sort out the struggle, the challenge, and the difficulty of transcending the ego. That sometimes requires some cajoling, sometimes a bit of pushing, and often just some gentleness. From the teacher's perspective, giving advice requires discernment, because he must be vigilant in ensuring that the guidance is not coming from his limited self.

Teachers serve as a catalyst for our change, and therefore the role of the teacher is to push the student to get past all the drama, tension, and patterns that are exposed. The teacher says, "Go through this. It hurts, but keep going." In effect, the teacher is pushing from the back and the power of God is pulling from the front, trying to bring about a real shift in our experience. It is only we who struggle because we do not recognize that what is fearful within is not the true Self. This drama gets played out repeatedly.

Sometimes we must simply have the courage to trust, and be willing to move through from one place to the next. The teacher can push, and God can pull—but the student has the ultimate power to persevere through difficult transitions. What is amazing is that on one level, transformation is so profoundly simple that once we do walk through a barrier we wonder, "What was all that fear about?"

The teacher must love each student unconditionally, yet the crust of each person needs to be dealt with in different ways. A teacher can help us burn karma, if we allow him to do so. But we need to ask for this help and we must mean it. Our karma is our karma—and while a teacher can provide us with the nourishment to free ourselves, he can't help free us of karma unless we ask him to, and unless we let go of that which binds us.

The great Tantric Buddhist Padmasambhava commented on the function aspect of the teacher-student relationship when he said, "There is nothing more useless than having a teacher whose guidance we follow on the condition that we agree with it." This means that when *śaktipāta* comes in the form of the word, we should not reject it just because we don't agree with it. I love this quote because it exposes a misconception in the mind of many students, who feel that accepting a teacher's guidance is an optional part of the relationship.

Instead of contracting or backing away when Grace comes in the form of advice, we must open and expand and create a new structure. By stretching past our boundaries we are strengthening our psychic mechanism so that we can hold more consciousness. We do that by first opening to the energy that comes through the words of the teacher, and then tuning in to the flow in ourselves and truly allowing that flow to carve an even bigger opening in us.

In some circumstances it is possible for a teacher to arouse that Divinity within us and support us as it unfolds, without talking to us. Nityananda rarely spoke, although sometimes he would throw coconuts at people! Thousands would stand in line to see him, and sometimes even if a person was some distance away, Nityananda would grab a coconut, throw it at him, and say, "Get out of here." How can we interpret this behavior? Perhaps the act of throwing a coconut was *śaktipāta* in action! The Divine Force flowing within Nityananda knew that this is what the person needed to wake up. As students, we really can't second-guess the intelligence behind the function, and that makes it challenging to understand this aspect of the teacher-student relationship. When do we listen and when do we not listen?

THE STUDENT'S RESISTANCE TO CHANGE

Inherent in our resistance to accepting the teacher's words is the fact that we are so attached to our limitations that we create a sophisticated array of diversionary strategies to avoid changing. If one tactic doesn't work, we try another. Maybe the fundamental tactic is denial. We say, "I don't need to be loved. I don't need to be nourished. I don't need help opening up." Holding this idea completely excludes us from the possibility of being nourished— from receiving the very Divine essence that is offered to us moment by moment—by the teacher and by the energy itself.

If the tactic of denial doesn't work, we arrogantly decide we can reject what the teacher is offering. We think, "I don't need God. I am whole in myself and don't need to let anyone in." The student's resistance to receiving is a major barrier for a teacher. Over time, as we experience the consistency of being loved, we do gain the courage to open. The teacher's love is really what frees us from the inability to receive. Perhaps the kindest thing any teacher can do is to reveal our ego to us. Maybe that is the highest form of love—but accomplishing this is not an easy job, especially if we resist receiving what is being offered.

Probably the most impenetrable barrier we have within ourselves, which keeps us from having a Divine Life, is our belief that we do not deserve it. This is the most insidious trick of the ego. When we think, "I don't deserve this," we are rejecting not only ourselves, but the life God gave us. We are denying the possibility of living in freedom. Why should we believe that all we deserve is misery?

The gift of Grace is about receiving. Although we talk a lot about the importance of giving, if we cannot receive, we will never be free. As the capacity to receive grows, the Grace of Divine Love frees us of everything that has been preventing us from opening even more deeply.

All of these forms of resistance become self-perpetuating. They become the reality we feed and therefore the reality from which we live our life. Our resistance becomes a magnet, establishing a resonance in everything we look at, feel, and touch. People are resistant to teachers because they don't want to trust. They don't trust themselves and they don't trust God, so they're certainly not going to trust the teacher. And perhaps an important part of the whole relationship is learning to find the willingness to trust somebody.

Only absolute unconditional trust in God will bring us liberation. Nothing short of that will. So having a teacher is practice for trusting God. We begin by accepting any frailty or fear we may feel inside, but we still make the commitment to build the strength to really open and let God in. It takes courage to let go of fear. It takes courage to change and to open to God. And the bottom line is we're so resistant to listening to a teacher precisely because we fear that he is going to say we need to change.

Often, the teacher's guidance is not easy to hear, so we sidestep the issue and say, "I should not have to hear this. I do not want to hear this." Usually, when we hear something about ourselves that we do not want to acknowledge, we reject it—even when we are sitting there burning inside, knowing it is right. We rationalize that it cannot be true. From the perspective of the teacher, this resistance creates much of the challenge and difficulty of teaching. So what is a student to do? What do we do with the function of the teacher? It is ultimately not the teacher we are surrendering to, not even to what they are saying. It is the act of surrender itself that serves us.

THE TEACHER AS A FIELD OF ENERGY

The third aspect of the teacher is serving as a field of energy, as a vehicle for transmission, or *śaktipāta*. I've said that *śaktipāta* is the descent of Grace, and that there are four traditional methods for transmission of energy—through look, touch, thought, and word. The challenge for students is to get beyond the misunderstanding that there is "Grace" and "not Grace" coming from the teacher. Is it Grace only when the teacher is giving direct transmission without words, or is it also available when he is talking and asking us to do something for ourselves? When a teacher says something to us, we get caught up in the words instead of recognizing that it's still the same force being transmitted.

In reality, all forms of *śaktipāta* are equally powerful in their potential to cut through a student's boundaries. Just as the function of the teacher is integrally related to the person of the teacher, the guidance function and *śaktipāta* are also entwined. In all dimensions of the relationship with the teacher, it is imperative that we remember that every part of our interaction with the teacher contains transmission.

When we accept somebody as a teacher, transmission happens on an ongoing basis, because the relationship is operating in a field of energy. It takes most students a long time to understand that this field does not function only in close proximity to the teacher.

We are engaging in a relationship with a living spiritual force that is always activated, and in one sense has nothing to do with either the person or the function of the teacher. My experience with Rudi, and certainly his experience with Nityananda, is proof that this dimension is alive—because even when the teacher is no longer in a human body, there is still a connection. This connection is a field of energy that we are part of, and which we consume at the same time that it consumes us. Truly, that spiritual force, and the love and nourishment within it, has the power to awaken the Divinity within us.

MY RELATIONSHIP WITH SWAMI CHETANANANDA

After Rudi died, I spent the next thirty years with Swami Chetanananda, and the three dimensions of the teacher were clearly evident for me in my relationship with him. It was an extraordinary relationship in every way, as it contained both nourishment and challenge. Part of the challenge was the fact that he was a person, and just as much of the challenge was the fact that he was not—that there was a powerful force at work in him that I had access to. Although the physical dimension of a teacher is clear, present, and inescapable in so many ways, the most important exchange between student and teacher happens on an energetic level. Trying to evaluate what part of the interaction derives from the person and their weakness and what is *śaktipāta* is ultimately not productive.

I stayed with Chetanananda because I recognized the power of the Grace that had been given to me by my teacher Rudi. And while I certainly recognized Rudi as my primary teacher, what some people might call a Sat Guru, I used my relationship with Chetanananda very consciously to gather the energy and support that was being offered to me, to further unfold the very thing that had been awakened in me by Rudi. I want to emphasize, however, that Chetanananda was my teacher for the thirty years that I lived in the ashram, and I lived in complete service, surrender, and devotion to him. That served him, and it served me. There is no greater treasure in this life than a teacher whom we can serve.

So many times in my relationship with Chetanananda, when I tried to separate the three dimensions of the teacher by saying, "This is the person speaking, and I am not going to accept this," I realized the resistance had been coming from a more limited part of me. As soon as I let go of that idea—let go of the resistance—what happened within me was a deeper opening, a bigger awareness, and more insight into my own limitations. So I learned to never lose sight of the powerful transformation that happens when one is engaged with a living spiritual force. We have to make the effort to engage and open to that energy field, deeply absorb it into ourselves, and allow it to nourish us, so that growth can take place.

Surrendering our attachment to our ego is a very subtle and tricky business. Be very thoughtful about trying to separate those dimensions when you start to think it is not the force but just the person working. Even our teacher's ego could be put in front of us to see if we are big enough to transcend it. Often my own experience was that what I thought was my teacher's ego, was not. It was mine. Even if it was his ego, it did not make a difference to me. It was the act of surrender that gave me what I needed, because in actuality, I never surrendered to him or his ego—I only surrendered to a deeper part of myself.

In other words, the real lesson was that having to work with both the physical teacher and the living force provided a powerful exercise in transcending duality. If you start trying to separate the three aspects of the teacher, you will pull and pull and you will never succeed.

KUNDALINI CALLS FORTH THE ENERGY IT NEEDS

When we are in a relationship with a teacher, *śaktipāta* takes whatever form is necessary to produce the needed effect in us. From my own experience with Rudi and Chetanananda, I can assure you that the cutting edge of their words was often much more powerful than any energy I might have felt in class. Those words carried a tremendous capacity to cut through my limitation and misunderstanding. And not once did I like the feedback—but every time, I was grateful for the opportunity to change and grow.

I like to call Rudi "the fastest sword in the West," because if you blinked from your clarity, from your center, or if you expressed your resistance, that sword came out. It was like a samurai movie in which two people are fighting and one of the combatants swings his sword. At first it appears that nothing has happened, and then suddenly the top half of someone's body tumbles. The amazing thing about Rudi was that he was always there to catch you before you hit the ground. He was there to love and hold you. Both the sword and the holding were forms of the same *śaktipāta*, that same powerful transmission.

Rudi's own experience with Swami Muktananda (one of Bhagavan Nityananda's key successors) was an example of how much one can receive from the energy force of a teacher despite some apparent limitation in the person. Rudi had tremendous respect for Muktananda, and at the same time felt there were some limitations in that teacher that interfered with their relationship. There are no perfect gurus. If they have a human body, they are imperfect. *Kuṇḍalinī* just calls forth the energy it needs and, fortunately or unfortunately, it comes in the form of a teacher for most people.

Our ability to recognize God in the teacher, and take the Grace that's flowing through them in spite of their apparent shortcomings, is part of the process of breaking down our own perception of duality. But you will definitely come up against parts of you that say, "I don't understand why he treats me this way, or doesn't treat me that way." We all find extraordinary resistance in our relationship to our teacher. The only issue is whether we allow our resistance to create fear and doubt, thereby undermining the very essence of the Grace being offered.

We hear some people say that they have a teacher in nonhuman form and they speak of a relationship with their "inner" teacher. In some ways this would be simpler, because one could sidestep the issues that arise when dealing with the limited, personal aspect of a human teacher. However, relying solely on our inner connection to a teacher, we lose the opportunity to receive truly objective feedback. It is all too easy to fool ourselves into believing what we want to believe, based on our own perspective, and then reinforce our misunderstandings by thinking they come from a non-embodied, inner teacher. We can thereby justify and perpetuate whatever limited understanding *we* have, all the while claiming it was our inner teacher who was guiding us. By doing this, we continually shortchange ourselves and avoid undertaking the serious, often difficult work that needs to be done if we really want to grow spiritually.

THE POWER OF THE ENERGY

Once a connection to a living teacher has been established, it is, however, quite possible to sustain and even deepen that relationship after the teacher is no longer physically present. Rudi knew Nityananda for just two years while the latter was alive. There are conflicting stories about how often Rudi was in his presence, but it was only one to five times. The exact number does not really matter, because the point is that Rudi's ongoing experience was with Nityananda in spirit form. Rudi continued to receive energetic transmissions from Nityananda and had palpable interchanges with him, even after this great saint took *mahāsamādhi* in 1961.

Similarly, although I knew Rudi for only sixteen months, the experience of him has continued to grow in me over the years. There has never been a moment that he has not been with me, except during the first thirty seconds after his death, when I could not find him. However, that was my problem, not a reflection of the potential to keep interacting with Rudi on a continuing basis. Rudi has been gone for nearly forty years and my relationship with him is a million times stronger now than it was at the time of his passing. The power of having a teacher is not restricted by proximity or physical form.

Some people believe that Nityananda never had a teacher, and perhaps he was one of those rare individuals who really did not need one. Nityananda was known for his spiritual attainment and was regarded as a teacher at a very young age. And yet there is a photograph of him sitting on the lap of Shivananda and clearly there was an extraordinary exchange happening there. We do not know whether Nityananda knew Shivananda for the three minutes he was sitting on his lap, or for three years, or even longer. Perhaps in just a brief meeting Shivananda provided a spark, which was all Nityananda needed to completely unfold what was already very highly developed within him. We will probably never know certain details about Nityananda's life. But if you are a person who truly does not need a teacher, you will know it.

The fundamental question each student has to ask is, "Will I achieve my liberation without a teacher?" It takes profound honesty to ask ourselves that question and really listen to the answer. Liberation comes from one place—and that is our direct and permanent experience of our connection to God. Any authentic teacher is attempting to help us establish this direct connection.

If our goal is realization, then we must decide whether we need a teacher in order to gain that experience. If you do need one, you will probably have to take the whole package. If you categorically know in your heart that your connection to God is complete, then you no longer need a teacher. And if the teacher is good, as soon as he sees that someone has that connection, he'll boot them out the door. Then they can just exchange postcards at Christmas. Sometimes we do not even need to ask if we're ready to leave, because we're like a ripe apple that simply falls off the tree. And sometimes we no longer need a teacher but do not know it yet—and all of a sudden, we find ourselves without one. The energy itself has orchestrated the end of the formal relationship. In this situation, what has really happened is that the student has consumed the teacher and his teachings completely.

A GOOD TEACHER WILL BE IN YOUR FACE

If you truly engage a teacher, it is one of the most difficult interactions you will ever have. A good teacher doesn't win popularity contests. His job is to free you, and you might not like or understand everything he does. This leads to the fun topic—your hate/love relationship with the teacher. If you don't sometimes hate your teacher, he is not doing his job. The following was written by Ken Wilber, a truly great teacher, author, and editor:

When it comes to spiritual teachers, there are those who are safe, gentle, consoling, soothing, caring; and there are the outlaws, the living terrors, the Rude Boys and Nasty Girls of God-realization, the men and women who are in your face, disturbing you, terrifying you, until you radically awaken to who and what you really are.

And may I suggest?: choose your teachers carefully.

If you want encouragement, soft smiles, ego stroking, gentle caresses of your self-contracting ways, pats on the back and sweet words of solace, find yourself a Nice Guy or Good Girl, and hold their hand on the sweet path of stress reduction and egoic comfort. But if you want Enlightenment, if you want to wake up, if you want to get fried in the fire of passionate Infinity, then, I promise you: find yourself a Rude Boy or a Nasty Girl, the ones who make you uncomfortable in their presence, who scare you witless, who will turn on you in a second and hold you up for ridicule, who will make you wish you were never born, who will offer you not sweet comfort but abject terror, not saccharine solace but scorching angst, for then, just then, you might very well be on the path to your own Original Face.

Most of us, I suspect, prefer our spiritual teachers to be one of the Nice-Guy variety. Soft, comforting, non-threatening, a source of succor for a worn and weary soul, a safe harbor in the samsaric storm. There is nothing wrong with that, of course; spirituality comes in all sorts of flavors, and I have known some awfully Nice Guys. But if the flavor tends towards Enlightenment instead of consolation, if it drifts away from soothing dreams toward actually waking up, if it rumbles toward a God realization and not egoic fortification, then that demands a brutal, shocking death: a literal death of your separate self, a painful, frightening, horrifying dissolution—a miraculous extinction you will actually witness as you expand into the boundless, formless, radical Truth that will pervade your every cell and drench your being to the core and expand what you thought was your self until it embraces the distant galaxies.

For only on the other side of death lies Spirit, only on the other side of egoic slaughter lies the Good, and the True and the Beautiful. "You will come in due course to realize that your true glory lies where you cease to exist," as the illustrious Sri Ramana Maharshi constantly reminded us. Your true glory lies on the other side of your death, and who will show you that?

Not the Nice Guys and not the Good Girls. They don't want to hurt your feelings. They don't want to upset you. They are here to whisper sweet nothings in your ear and place consolation prizes in the outstretched hand of the self-contraction, balm for a war-torn weary ego, techniques to prop it up in its constant battle with the world of otherness. In a sense, it's very easy being a Nice-Guy teacher: no muss, no fuss, no wrestling with egoic resistance and exhausting confrontation. Be nice to the ego, pat it on the back, have it count its breaths, hum a few mantras.

Rude Boys know better. They are not here to console but to shatter, not to comfort but to demolish. They are uncompromising, brutal, laser-like. They are in your face until you recognize your Original Face—and they simply will not back off, they will not back down, they will not let up until you let go—radically, fully, completely, unhesitatingly. They live as Compassion—real compassion, not idiot compassion—and real compassion uses a sword more often than a sweet. They deeply offend the ego (and the greater the offense, the bigger the ego). They are alive as Truth, they are everywhere confronted with egos, and they choose the former uncompromisingly . . .

So, can you stand the heat? Or would you like more soft and consoling words of comfort, more consolation prizes for an Enlightenment that will continue to elude you? Would you like a pat on the back, or are you ready to be skinned and fried?

May I suggest this? If you can stand the heat, you will indeed come to realize that your true glory lies where you cease to exist, where the self-contraction has uncoiled in the vast expanse of all space, where your separate self has been roasted and replaced by infinity resplendent—a radical Release much too obvious to see, much too simple to believe, much too near to be attained—and your real Self will quietly but surely announce its Presence as it calmly embraces the entire universe and swallows galaxies whole . . .

If you can stand the heat, then enter the real kitchen of your own soul, where you will find nothing other than the radiant God of the entire cosmos. For it is radiant Spirit that is looking out from your eyes right now, speaking with your tongue right now, reading the words on this very page, right now. Your real Self is glorious Spirit in this and every moment, and it takes a very, very Rude Boy to point that out and to stay in your face until you recognize your own Original Face, shining even here and now.

It is even possible to have a teacher whose values we really do not respect, yet we can still receive nourishment from him and can continue to surrender to the energy. Throughout history this has been done many times. Did it always work? Maybe, maybe not. Only you can decide if you have the inner strength—or rather, if going through that process will create the inner strength for that type of relationship. Many scriptures talk about how inscrutable the teacher is . . . but scripture is generally written by teachers!

CONSUMING THE TOTALITY OF THE TEACHER

If the teacher isn't serving you and your freedom, they're not your teacher. It is certainly important for a student to recognize whether the teacher is living from the control and arrogance of power, or from the love and humility of service. If any teacher we happen to study with isn't serving God, ultimately they will end up serving themselves, which means they can't serve us. Although this represents a valid reason to leave a teacher, we must be very careful not to interpret their service through our egoic filter. We may easily close down instead of opening to the very teaching we need in order to get beyond our own perspective—so we have to be very quiet inside in order to evaluate this. We have to ask, "Am I being freed?" If we hold on to a preconceived idea of what a perfect guru should be, we may wait a very long time before we find one.

As Rudi said, "Life must be consumed whole with all its pain, joy, and sorrow." This maxim can also be applied to our relationship to a teacher. Every aspect of the teacher must be consumed, including his ego. And that is how we free ourselves from a teacher—by consuming him. We have to trust that all that is pure in essence will stay in us, and that which is not will leave. If we can trust ourselves and can trust God, then we can probably trust our teacher.

The teacher is a multidimensional well from which students drink as they choose. As a teacher, if a student asks my advice, I will give it—generally fairly unattached, knowing that the student often will not listen. If someone does not want or does not act on my advice, I do not take it personally. A student must become like the hamsa bird, a mythical creature that has a unique talent. If milk and water are mixed together, the bird can extract the milk from the mixture, and then can extract the sweetness from the milk. This is how we use the teacher: we absorb what we need to grow and throw out all the rest. Just be sure to drink deeply from all dimensions, and do not discard the remains too soon.

In the presence of the teacher, the miracle of transmission happens by God's Grace. We receive this Grace through contact with the living spiritual force that is accessible to us in our teacher. This is what we should pay attention to and hold on to. But understand that even when we receive the extraordinary nourishment of *śaktipāta*, the transmission is only half the equation of arousing the Divinity. The other part of our work involves the dissolution of the ego, and therefore we must deal with the fierce battle it puts up to prevent that dissolution. This is where the function of guidance is so important.

An important question always arises when discussing the relationship with a living teacher who has physical form, which is: Do we surrender to the teacher? And the answer is: Never. We only surrender *through* the teacher. We only surrender to what the teacher surrenders to. We only trust what the teacher trusts. But will attunement to that ultimate surrender take the specific form of some interaction with that person? Absolutely.

However, having said that we only surrender within ourselves, sometimes surrendering to a teacher is the form in which we find an internal place of surrender. In that case, we do respond to the Grace being offered in this form, but understand that the person is not the source. The force of Grace simply flows through the teacher. This is an interesting discussion for my students because it sounds like I'm talking about myself. But I'm aware it has nothing to do with me. I'm merely the vehicle for the flow of Grace, and I take it as a profound responsibility. Every day, I try to get out of the way so that Grace flows through in as pure a form as possible.

A Living Spiritual Force

The fact that Grace generally comes through a person is not relevant, unless we make it so. Rudi told of his own meeting with Nityananda in Ganeshpuri in 1959. As he walked into a bare room with just a single light bulb hanging there, Rudi saw what he described as a giant of a man — and Nityananda was very short, so it wasn't the physical form that was impressive. While looking across the room Nityananda's gaze caught Rudi's eye and in one moment of transmission Rudi's life was transformed. Just through that gaze. It was the recognition of the power inherent in this type of transmission that inspired Rudi to teach open-eyes class.

This moment was the catalytic point in Rudi's life. He was like a camel coming to a well. Rudi's spiritual practices had begun at a very early age, and although he was only about thirty when he met Nityandanda, Rudi had worked extremely hard for many years. It was the work he had already done that attracted to him the vital force of energy that was Nityananda. But it was really during the subsequent twelve to fourteen years, after Nityananda's *mahasamādhi*, that the relationship between Rudi and Nityananda became vivid.

Although their relationship started while Nityananda had a physical form, the transmission of energy has nothing to do with the physical person or the physical body. Nityananda never sat down and taught a formal class. If you were within a hundred miles, you were in class—or within ten thousand miles, once you'd made initial contact.

I consider myself extremely fortunate, because my initial encounter with Rudi was so powerful that it changed the trajectory of my life. In that sense this meeting was not much different from Rudi's experience with Nityananda. The only distinction is that Rudi had spent years of ardent practice to prepare for his meeting and I had spent years of non-practice! It was Grace that suddenly awakened in me a desire to know God, and that energy then attracted my teacher.

What would my life have been like if Rudi had stayed alive for another thirty years? I don't know. I can only imagine it would have been amazing—and yet profoundly more intense and difficult at the same time. Despite his having died in 1973, my relationship with Rudi has grown infinitely since then, especially in the years since I moved to Berkeley. And through Rudi I have a very strong connection with Nityananda, because that energy is a living spiritual force that gets transmitted from a teacher to a student, who may become a teacher, and so on, down through the generations. The energy itself selects some particular physical form that it might manifest through, and that's its choice.

If realization is our goal in life, we must be very thoughtful about what we need in order to achieve it. Only you know within yourself when you make contact with a teacher or a practice whether it is going to serve you or not. My advice is to find one that opens your heart and become a master in it. If your heart starts to close again, don't reject the teaching. Give it time to produce a lasting transformation.

A teacher is part of the Grace of our lives, of our own Divinity trying to free us from ourselves. The greatest act of service a teacher can perform is to expose to us our limitation, and at the same time reveal that which is not limited. Engaging in a relationship with a teacher gives us contact with a living spiritual force that can nourish our spiritual development. With this help, we dissolve the tensions that block the unfolding of Divinity, so that we can find the full expression of God within ourselves. That is the purpose of having a teacher. I say it again: There is no greater treasure in this life than having a relationship with an authentic teacher.

THE ALCHEMY OF
SELFLESS SERVICE

7

CHAPTER SEVEN

Grace is a gift from God. We have been given the opportunity to know and love the Divine—to experience a lifetime of growth and celebration. In return, we offer our gratitude and selfless service. Selfless service, or *seva*, comes from an open heart and is centered in a profoundly simple place within. The desire to serve arises from the merging of our heart with the heart of God, in a state of complete surrender. Selfless service is simply the natural expression of the love, gratitude, and devotion we feel. We can't help but think, "How can I give back to the life that has given me this joy?" Nityananda expressed this beautifully when he said, "As is your devotion, so is your liberation." Service is a reflection of the awareness we connect to in ourselves and what we express in our actions. We serve because it frees us to know our Divinity.

Our ego keeps us from this Self-knowledge, and it is fear of losing ourselves that keeps the ego functioning. We live in a box, which defines our life in many ways. We get trapped in patterns, thinking, "This is what my life is. This is what I can or can't do, and this is what I will or won't do." If we wish to extend past these preconceptions, we must exert some effort to break free, because we all carry a resistance and an unwillingness to change. We must huff and puff and blow our own walls down, and not accept the smallness.

One of the primary ways we can knock the walls down is by deciding to truly give of ourselves—and to do so when it's wanted and needed and especially when we don't want to give. But we *do* give, because it expands our boundaries. It really requires that we open our hearts more. Isn't this what we say we want? We get past our limitations when we serve and surrender.

The restructuring of our consciousness involves finding a deeper inner awareness, tuning in and feeling it in ourselves, and then extending it outward from our center. When we serve somebody, we are allowing the openness we found inside to expand and make contact with another person. This is how we nourish them. We are creating a flow with our own life in whatever situation we encounter. It is sometimes difficult to feel the flow in ourselves, and it is sometimes a challenge to connect the flow with our life. We have to really extend past ourselves. This is not different from our inner practice, but now we are stretching into the world, and this interaction takes the form of offering love and service.

Surrender and service are the easiest things to do if we open our hearts and tune in to the Divine. Then it is not even "you" giving but simply Divinity flowing through you, shedding light on everything. Living beyond desire and attachment does not mean we do not care. Be passionate when you care about something. Be passionate from an open heart and with an open hand. This is the foundation from which we can really serve, because we are not concerned about what we are going to get in return. The work of a liberated person is simply to give, and we can only do this when we have freed ourselves from the selfishness of our own need.

Dissolving Our Boundaries

The experience of living in the flow of life and energy dissolves all sense of something "happening to me." It dissolves duality itself—the sense that there is "me" and something "other." As we grow, we continually reach into the experience that there is unity in life, and yet part of us retains the feeling of separation.

To create a more permanent connection with the Divine, we make an effort to reach deeper inside. We meditate more, and at the same time learn to extend past our boundaries, past the place where we feel the discontinuity between the Unity within and the loss of that Unity when we engage the world. It is through service that we start to dissolve our separation, those subtle veils of duality.

The concept of service can be boiled down to one simple statement: Selfless service is about giving what is wanted and needed and not what we want to give. That is exactly why it breaks down our boundaries, because in order to really give what is needed, we have to get past our limitations. We have to get beyond the resistance to giving.

Service requires us to open up and push through these boundaries, using the power of flow. What happens when we do that? We get bigger—which is the prerequisite of moving from an awareness of life as energy to experiencing life as pure Presence. We begin to move into a state where our identity is dissolved, and we can have a life that is simply an expression of consciousness, of higher awareness. That is a good reason to break down our boundaries. So although selfless service is getting past ourselves and giving to others, we are, in fact, the ultimate recipient.

In the state of non-duality, there is no concept of, "I will give here, but I won't give there," or "I won't give this or that part of me." The work is to give from the state of pure Oneness and pure understanding of the unity of life. We must become the consciousness we seek. In other words, we have to give from a place of unconditionality in order to experience unconditionality. How can we ever experience this if we function from condition? It is not possible. So in a sense we are expanding beyond our capacity to understand. The fact that our life is requesting that we function on a higher level is an extraordinary gift.

I've said that service comes from an open heart. If the heart is filled with stuff, then it is not open. It does not matter where the obstructions came from, who put them there, or why they are there. The issue is whether we leave them lodged inside us. If we open our heart all the blocks dissolve. It is truly within each person's capacity to reach a state of openness at any moment, if our wish is profound enough. We seek to completely transcend our problems and fears—to live in a state of simply loving God. It is our ability to not only have that experience but to translate it into action that is the true test of our understanding of, and our commitment to, living in openness.

SERVING THE DIVINE

Service is transcending our personal needs and expressing a devotion and love for God that allows us to surrender to Divine Will. So often, when we hear a statement like that we immediately get nervous. Our reaction is, "What do you mean? I have to give up what I want?" However, that is not what the statement implies. It simply means that we have to transcend our preconceived ideas about what our personal needs are. In surrendering to Divine Will we may get what we want or we may not. The critical issue is this: Are we able to transcend our preconceptions and live from a state of fulfillment even if we do not end up having the things we *think* we want and need? There is, as Mick Jagger points out, a very important distinction between getting what we want and getting what we need.

We are always serving the Divine. We are serving the freedom that already exists within us, opening to the Divinity that is trying to express Itself through us. And although there will be many times when we don't want to serve, the issue is whether we dwell in our resistance or use the opportunity to move past our own boundaries. We learn to get beyond tuning in to our private radio station KAMAT—"All Me, All the Time"—and dial in to KGOD,

"All God, All the Time." That's why we serve, regardless of the situation. We do it because we made a choice for liberation, and there is one guarantee that comes with our wish to serve—that we will have exactly what we need to provide us the opportunity for growth.

If devotion and service are part of the path of finding God, we cannot expect to go down that road without having to get a little bit bigger than we currently are. We should trade our own narrow understanding of what we want and need in this life for the profound magnificence of what is available to us. Which one do we choose? All too often we attach ourselves to our perceived needs, give life to them, and spend the rest of our lives trying to justify and fulfill our desires. We have such limited capacity to imagine what is possible for us that we attach ourselves to the most meaningless pursuits, thinking they will give us fulfillment. These pursuits are not inherently bad, but in chasing them we don't allow the magnificence of Divine Grace to penetrate into our awareness.

TRANSCENDING OUR NEEDS AND ATTACHMENTS

People get so caught up in the most idiotic, mundane tensions. The mantra of stupidity, coined by Swami Chetanananda, is "What's gonna happen to me?" All tension arises from this incessant focus. We are so busy worrying about what is going to happen to us that we completely lose the ability to see the infinite potential in our lives. It is that simple—and yet we have to work at understanding and unfolding this within ourselves. We work to transcend our personal needs, to transcend our tensions, to transcend what we think is real.

If we cannot trust the Divine we will never get close to seeing beyond our needs—because without that trust we will continually live in the fear of losing something. We will never get beyond this limitation. Trusting the Divine does not mean writing affirmations on the chalkboard a million times until we finally believe it. We must feel it in our hearts, and refuse to accept not feeling it. We reach and reach inside, we surrender and open deeper until we do. Established in this contact with the Divine, living a life of devotion and service is profoundly simple because we recognize that we always have everything we need.

Sometimes we find ourselves thinking, "I don't want to do this. I don't have time, I'm too tired, I have a headache, why should I have to do this when other people don't have to?" These thoughts are the surface manifestation of a deeper issue. They are simply the ego expressing its self-absorbed focus. We are really exposing our attachment to our identity, which is camouflaged by all of our needs and misunderstandings. So we step up and serve, because it enables us to work at the deepest level—to work on the dissolution of our separate identity, which is the goal of spiritual practice. And we keep giving until we do understand, "Oh, this is why I needed to do this."

We constantly give our tensions reality. We build excuses to explain why we have them, and then we start to rationalize the excuses themselves—and it's an endless mind trip. It is only in our hearts that we can transcend this cycle. We all have had the experience of agonizing over some tension and then at some point we let go and it is gone. Part of the challenge is to recognize that our hopes and dreams may in fact be our own illusions. By holding on to these aspirations we miss sight of reality. When we let go of them we can begin to serve something higher in ourselves.

At times, even when we desire to serve the highest, it is still easy to slip into "What will happen to me?" The reason it becomes so hard to distinguish between the two is that when our small self starts wanting things, and we start working hard to give that part of us what it needs, we forget completely about the more profound dimensions of life. We are an individuated expression of Divine Oneness. Fully experiencing that expression is why we can have an individuated life and all the accoutrements that go with it. So let's celebrate it. But let's not forget that the reason we have this life in the first place is to know the highest part of ourselves.

THE COST OF SERVICE AND LIBERATION

You need to be honest with yourself. What if liberation *was* something you could buy and you had a billion dollars. Would you invest it in your freedom, as opposed to the twenty-five-bedroom house on your own private island? How would you use the billion? Would you give it right back if you thought it could buy freedom? Most of us might not.

It is hard to imagine what we have not experienced—and that is one of the reasons why our growth is so elusive. It is only when we are very still inside that we begin to get a glimpse of what freedom means. Transcending our personal needs takes courage, commitment, and being prepared to sacrifice. Maybe you will never have to sacrifice, but whether or not you are prepared to do so is the real issue.

Selfless service, however, is not about donating money. It is not a question of being charitable in that sense. If someone has 20 million dollars, and gives 2 million to Save the Something Foundation, it costs them nothing—and while it may be generous, it is not service.

Authentic service is to the Divine, allowing Grace to emerge from within us, thereby fulfilling God's desire to experience Himself through us. Transforming ourselves into an instrument of God is truly an act of selfless service. The practice or *sādhana* of serving the God within us must start from that depth of awareness. When we open and function on this basis, our capacity to give something of true value to others will be extraordinary.

SERVICE AND KARMA

From the perspective of Tantric practice there is a conscious reason we serve, and this involves the issue of karma, which is the creation or repetition of pattern. It is understood that freeing ourselves of karma is necessary for our liberation, and truly serving from a selfless point of view is *the* action that does not create more karma. To allow the cycle of death and rebirth to be dissolved, there are two things we have to do—burn up the karma we've already created, and not create more. If we are serving to dissolve our karmic bonds, are we being selfish? It depends on how you look at it. Ultimately, we're not serving the world; we're serving the Source of the world. Karma limits our ability to unshackle the God within, and therefore the seemingly selfish goal of transcending our karma fulfills a higher purpose.

Through service we may be able to avoid creating new karma, but what happens when our past karma shows up in the form of a person? Again, we serve and engage the situation from a selfless perspective. Instead of responding from the limited viewpoint that created the karma in the first place, we selflessly extend ourselves back into the dynamic. In so doing we not only free ourselves, but we free others of that interchange. After all, they were in the boxing ring with us in the first place! And it's selfless because we don't go back and allocate blame, as we usually do.

Quite often we dig a deeper karmic binding by holding on to past patterns, past-life energy trapped in the horizontal. This only entangles us deeper. The people and the karmic situations that come into our lives surface for one reason—to free everyone from the repeated cycle. If we engage people with this understanding we'll have a very different perspective on what the reality and the point of that relationship is. And even more importantly, we won't get caught in what we need from someone else.

UNCONDITIONAL GIVING

We don't say, "Here, let me love you and serve you so I can get what I need." We simply serve people, and we become very passionate about that engagement from a position of openness and consciousness rather than from a place of emotional need. And if someone doesn't want to be served we don't persist in trying to bludgeon them with what we think they need. It can certainly be painful to watch people wreck their lives by making what appear to be poor decisions—but unless they specifically ask us to intervene, we have no right to do so. Somehow, we assume we have that right. If we are engaging in truly selfless service, we have no agenda and no desire to benefit from our actions.

Part of *seva* is acknowledging the God that is in each of us, and knowing that we serve this inner Divinity. But if loving God is expressed by truly giving to others, why is it that we can't offer what they ask for? Often we don't know the difference between what we want to give and what they really want. The closer people are to us, the bigger challenge it is to serve them. I am not saying to walk out the door, meet people, and give each one what they ask for. That is not our responsibility. It does, however, require profound discrimination and awareness to overcome our judgment about what another person does or does not need. We must listen, ask, and be very careful and quiet about this.

It takes work to be conscious, and service happens from the heart, not from the mind. We have to feel into a situation, go inside, and really ask for clarity. We may not always be able to give people exactly what they want and need, but at least that is what we focus on. If we are really looking to see what is needed in a situation, we can never be diminished in the process. We only become bigger. If we find ourselves feeling diminished, that's a signal to get quiet inside and ask, "Am I really serving, or am I just deluding myself? Am I functioning from a simple place, or expressing my own needs?"

All too often, we serve, or choose not to serve, from insecure places or from fear. When we surrender our life to serving the Divine, we are absorbed in God's love and witness its expression. Immersed in Oneness, we act from a platform of unconditional loving and giving. It is love that allows us to express our devotion in the form of sacrificing the demands of our small self.

KNOWING WHAT TO GIVE

However, we may still have the thought, "What if I'm asked to give something I shouldn't have to give?" What do we do then? We should be a little suspect of the part of us that thinks, "I shouldn't have to give this." If God dwells within us and expresses Himself as *our* life, then what is being asked of us always comes from the same Divinity. How many of us can realistically argue with God when He says, "Here I am, now do this for me"? Instead of turning down that request, we learn to recognize that this is what is happening every day. The Divinity within us is expressing Itself externally, saying, "Give me this."

On the other hand, let's suppose you have a brother who is an alcoholic. To continue to buy alcohol for him would be a disservice. What he says he wants may not be what he really needs. At such times, love can provide the lens through which we discern when God is asking us to serve Him, and when it is some person's weakness or ego demanding attention. We will all find situations in which everything in us completely rails against giving what is being asked for. We have to be very careful to evaluate this impulse, because it may in fact be of service to back off when we question what a person needs from us.

It is when a situation reveals that we do not want to change that we must become alert to the fact that our own weakness is being exposed. Then, we have to break ourselves down in order to give what we know clearly needs to be given—and sometimes, to stop trying to take what we have been taking.

Teachers face a similar issue of having to discern what to give. Sometimes when a student is going through a lot of pain, and they want you to attempt to end their distress, the greatest disservice would be to do that. The truth of the matter is that for his long-term growth, a student may need to deal with a situation himself. The teacher's role is to help the student unfold the Divinity within himself, not necessarily to make him feel better or more comfortable.

A teacher is serving God, not individual students—helping that force emerge, wherever and however it wants to show itself. Of course, in the process of serving God, it frequently happens that the teacher is serving a specific person as well. But the teacher does not choose whom to serve, and the student does not get to dictate the exact form of that service.

THE INTERNAL ENERGY OF SERVICE

As we really learn to serve, we start to expose where we are serving from, as well as why we are serving. Surrender is about diminishing and transcending the limited self, giving something that initially we do not yet know how to give. We have to find a way to give something of ourselves that is beyond our current capacity. Although stretching in this way opens us up, it doesn't necessarily make us feel better. Sometimes giving what is wanted makes us feel worse. It's hard, and we deal with dense energies that take a lot of work to process.

When we are serving someone with emotional baggage and it starts to affect us, we have to understand what is happening and transmute that dense energy into the flow inside. We do this by using the double-breath to internalize the energy. It may not be easy and it may really tax us, but it will definitely allow us to grow if we say, "I will do this. I will get big enough and find a way to process this energy." Dealing with this type of intense energy should simply be regarded as something to digest, like a gourmet meal. We don't have to engage the situation—but if we've chosen to, it will serve our growth as well as the dynamic in our life. So often when we've been resisting giving in some way and finally do it, it may cost us, but that service fulfills a need in someone else.

In serving we may go through a demanding experience that feels like running the gauntlet of a hazing line in boot camp. It's hard getting through, but we're elated when we get to the other end of it. Our heart is open, we're grateful we did it, and we recognize what it did for us. A conscious person would line up again—because by repeatedly serving in this way, a real shift in awareness will occur and we will start functioning from an entirely different place. I've said that we should serve to find our Self, but too often we do not function from that perspective. If we serve but moan and groan about it the whole time, we will get nothing out of it.

LEARNING TO SERVE THE HIGHEST IN OURSELVES

It takes a long time to understand the foundation of service—that we are not serving anybody or anything, but simply serving the Divinity that happens to express itself in these forms. There is a parable in which Jesus is knocking on people's doors asking for food, and nobody recognizes him. Unfortunately, we get caught in the dualistic position of, "Why should I have to serve that situation or serve that person?" We miss the point of *seva*—which is to become selfless! It is said that God's favorite name for Himself is "The servant of servants." For humans, service involves emptying ourselves of our limited perspective and understanding so that our own Divinity and freedom can show itself.

When we experience resistance to serving someone right in front of us, why not take a magic marker and write "God" on his forehead? Then perhaps we can find the capacity to say, "I won't serve him, but I'll serve God." The wonderful thing about *seva* is that it is unconditional, so even if a little voice comes up, saying that people do not appreciate what we are giving, we still continue to serve.

Serving is a field of awareness we find within ourselves, from which we can function. We can also use it as a barometer of our growth. Whenever we find ourselves caught up in our own limitations, we should stop and ask, "Wait a minute, didn't I make a commitment to live selflessly?" We do not start climbing a mountain unless we have the intention of reaching the top; otherwise, we will stop at the fancy resort halfway up. But we cannot suddenly arrive at the top of Mount Everest. We must make the climb. So we start with selfless service as the goal, learning what it means to serve as we progress along that path.

The essential question to consider when evaluating our commitment to service is, "Am I serving the highest in me through my actions? Am I liberating the Divine within me?" When we have the courage to ask in these terms, it helps us make a lot of decisions. We learn that the service we do in the world, for our spiritual community, for our teacher, and for the people we know, is all building the muscle, the capacity to ask that question and to eventually answer, "Yes." Service is not something separate from our life. We don't live our spiritual life in one dimension and then serve "over there."

Every aspect of our life is integrated and everything we practice helps to transform us, to crack the walls of duality. Often this change requires a bit of force, and we need help to get past our boundaries. Serving can allow a plan to be revealed to us that is in our highest and best interest—and I think we can all accept that our own plans are not always in our highest interest. The ability to truly serve in a detached way, without needing a reward or a response, is beginning to say to God, "Thy will be done. May my will be Your will."

SELFLESSLY SERVING, SELFLESSLY RECEIVING

When is it that we *really* serve? We all find it easy to serve when we want to, when our hearts are open and we are filled with gratitude and devotion. However, there are two other times we must serve: when we do not want to, and when we have discovered that what we thought we were doing as service was not really serving at all—we were only serving ourselves. Then we become serious about whether we're willing to selflessly serve. It's a precipice, an opportunity to truly understand it. I suggest that each of you will come to that moment at least once in your life. And once is all it really takes.

I can share an example of this in my own life. A number of years ago, I exposed a profoundly deep pattern of self-service in myself. It wasn't pretty, but instead of being caught up in the specifics of what happened, I understood that there was something really entrenched being exposed, and that is what I focused on. A powerful revelation occurred one night when I woke up having an incredibly intense experience. It felt like I was hanging on a massive stone wall, tied up by iron shackles around my ankles and outstretched arms. The atmosphere was dark and dank, like a dungeon. A parade of people came by, and one would take a big stick and whack me . . . the next person would burn me . . . the next flayed me with a knife . . . and so it went.

What I understood throughout this experience was that these were the people from this and past lifetimes whom I had hurt by my pattern of self-serving. At the end of this encounter with person after person, the only part of me that survived was my eyes. Everything else had been obliterated. The eyes remained to see—so that I could really absorb what was being shown to me.

This was not fun. It was downright ugly. Yet the experience was powerfully liberating, because there was something that had to be exposed in order for me to find freedom from that particular pattern. The self-serving pattern had been so deeply veiled that I had not been aware of it until then. Although this story may sound frightening, in the middle of my experience there was also profound sweetness—but only because I was able to shift my consciousness and focus on wanting to understand, to look and see what was being shown to me. If I had gotten caught up in all the manifestation the pattern created, or the pain of having it exposed, then I would not have understood what was really going on. Instead, I was able to deeply understand what I needed to change in myself in order to continue my growth.

Who would want that kind of experience? But do we need it? Yes. We need to have our powerful patterns of karma and tension dissolved, and it is Grace that makes this happen. The first act of Grace is to give us a gift—which may be an uplifting and blissful gift or one that is challenging to our own unconsciousness. Then it is up to us to do our work. We must choose to receive what God gives us for our freedom.

We must open and change based on what we are being asked to change. Otherwise we miss that opportunity. But this is the power of the ego—to reject even what God is trying to show us. It is vital that you understand what it is you are seeking. Understand the depth of wish required to achieve that goal and the transformation you will have to go through in order to attain it. We must learn our lessons when they are given, receiving whatever messages God sends, whenever he chooses to send them, even if they aren't easy to digest. God is not a white-haired guy with big fluffy wings. Sometimes he is red and has horns! True service has no pattern to it, and growing spiritually is a perilous choice. If we are not devoted to our freedom, we will not make that choice.

Reaching the juncture where we are ready to begin serving selflessly is a cause for celebration. All the service we'd been doing up until then was essentially priming the pump, getting us to the point when we truly see ourselves. It is in that moment, when we realize we were not being selfless, that we must step up and access a deeper, unconditional willingness to serve. This is when we can really change and become bigger. So we serve as best we can until we get to that point, and then decide what we want to do about reaching a deeper level of service.

Don't ever let there be a conflict in your mind between serving and growing. Serving and growing are the same. If we do not grow, we will not serve because we will not have the capacity to do so. This is why we start with the person next to us and try to serve them deeply—because it forces us to grow. One trap many people face is that they extend their energy and constantly give and give, so they do not have to face themselves and change. In this case they may be doing something for someone, but they are not really serving others, or themselves. They are not growing in the process, but are acting from some mask of the ego, to protect something within them. If we are really serving, it is going to expose our agendas.

Sometimes, it seems that in a thousand hours of service, only a small fraction is really an expression of selfless service—and yet, experiencing this state of selflessness is incredible. We know why we are serving, and we work to be in that space again, to create that permanent immersion into selflessness. We get glimpses of it, or even big shots of it, and then it fades away. Moving in and out of that awareness is the process we go through, and we continue to work every day until we are firmly established in a higher place.

We all have some experience of feeling a profound love in ourselves and sincerely wanting to expand that and serve a higher purpose. But somehow, between the time we have that experience and the time we walk out our door, we lose the awareness. Rudi spoke of this as the test of our life.

When we find love within ourselves, the question becomes: Can we translate it into action? Most of what we do is an extension of our restricted, lower self—the part of us that does not experience Oneness. We can't help but reflect that in our actions. When we function from the state of Oneness, there is no individual remaining, and therefore no limitation to our consciousness or our ability to express a higher awareness in action. If we wish to transform our awareness, we must serve and experience selflessness, because this is what takes us beyond duality.

In time, what gets revealed to us is that the flip side of selfless service is the capacity to selflessly receive. Even if service exhausts us, we recognize that we are receiving something much deeper in return. We learn to move past our attachment to our actions or to our situation in life, and are open to receiving whatever God wants to give. Giving and receiving are inseparable.

The capacity to live in simplicity is the fruit of truly understanding the incredible effulgence and magnificence of God's own intelligence, and allowing it to express itself in our life. We are letting God show Himself through the life He has designed for us.

Our individuated growth is the most profound act of selfless service because we are allowing the Divine to emerge from within us, and this fulfills the very purpose for which God created our life. Wanting to know God is not an act of selfishness. The reality is that it is only God wanting to know Himself. When we surrender our life to serving the Divine, we are absorbed in the expression of Divine Love and can fully receive Divine Grace. We are immersed in and surrendered to the unity of life. We must embrace this ultimate field of awareness if we want our realization, and it is from this depth of consciousness that true selfless service is possible.

Conscious Choice & Disciplined Action

8

CHAPTER EIGHT

Conscious choice and disciplined action are linked together as one of the key means of transformation because this is how we decide whether or not we are going to live a spiritual life. When we choose to live this life, we are making the decision to spiritualize our life force. We draw this force within us, and instead of allowing it to be expressed in the ordinary dimension of life, we consciously and constantly reinvest it—internalizing the energy back into ourselves to release the Spirit within.

Growing spiritually is a completely conscious choice we must make every day, moment by moment. But choosing is only half of the equation. The discipline to stay within ourselves, remain in contact with our center, and extend this inner power into life is what enables that choice to result in a real transformation of awareness and experience.

Living an extraordinary life can be defined as gaining access to the Divine Power within us—feeling and being aware of the Divine at all times, as the pulsation that gives us life. In addition, we must focus on living the life God gave us instead of the one we are always trying to fabricate. We have an amazing capacity to romanticize, fantasize, and believe our life is somewhere else. Our life is here, right now, every single day. Are we going to live in the drama and suffering we create or in the simplicity and unconditional joy available to us? We must recognize how incredible life is, as it is. When we constantly choose to focus on an imaginary "better" life, we deny ourselves the ability to experience what is right in front of us.

THE BATTLEFIELD OF TRANSFORMATION

Scripture often talks about the spiritual hero, the person who wins on the battlefield of his own life. If we do not choose to grow every day, we will not live as a hero. The classic example of a spiritual warrior is Arjuna, the hero of the Bhagavad Gita. He is faced with deciding whether to go into battle, knowing that the people he will have to fight and kill are his brothers, cousins, and other relatives.

In the process of coming to grips with this seemingly impossible situation, Arjuna learns that the real "battle" to be fought is within him. There is a powerful line in which Lord Krishna says that a man who defeats a thousand of his enemies is a great man—but a man who defeats himself is greater. The whole point of the war, and of the lesson, was not how many people Arjuna defeated. The real question was whether he could defeat his wrong understanding about life and his own nature.

It is in this sense that we describe life as a battlefield. Every situation we encounter is there for one reason—to enable us to rise above it and thereby free us of some misunderstanding or limitation within ourselves. And often this freedom is obtained through considerable hard work.

Certainly Rudi experienced his life as a minefield, and from his perspective his life was one continuous battle. Yet he worked and found profound joy in himself regardless of the difficulty. He did not say, "Only when I get through the work will I be happy." He discovered happiness within himself, and this is what we all must do.

FEEDING OUR CHOICE

Growing is not easy and it is not normal, in the sense that few people choose to make growth a priority in life. I have done this practice since 1971 and, like Rudi, I have worked hard. Certain things are easy for me now that may be difficult for beginners. As spiritual practice develops over time, when we deeply center ourselves inside, it becomes easier to choose whether or not to engage a particular tension or situation. As our consciousness and awareness grow, we gain an understanding of what hooks us in life and what does not—and then we can consciously choose to rise above any situation.

When we ask to grow, we must not only be conscious of what we are choosing, but we must also develop the awareness to know if we are really feeding the highest in ourselves. What grows in us is what we feed. If we feed our need, it grows. If we feed our desire to be rich, or to be fulfilled by having a partner, then this is what will grow. We must realize that although our focus may intensify a specific need, satisfying any particular desire will not necessarily bring fulfillment.

Many people tell me they have a desire to engage in some creative activity, often equating this with fine or expressive arts. They say this type of creativity is their spiritual practice. My response is this: The most extraordinarily creative thing we can do is transform ourselves and realize our own true nature. We should love life, engage it fully, and look for creative expression—but the highest expression of creative potential we can focus on is the unfolding of our own freedom. We cannot reject any aspect of life, and yet we do have to make choices. The fundamental conscious question is, "Will this support my spiritual growth?" Sometimes the hardest things to do are those that support growth, and the easiest are the things that do not.

In order for our inner life to grow, it has to be fed and nourished. Growth must be what we choose to focus on every day. And although we speak in terms of life being a battlefield and emphasize that we must be committed to doing the work, our growth needs to be a joyous undertaking. If we cannot find the joy and the incredible, extraordinary awareness within that work, then we will stop pursuing our spiritual growth.

The prize is enormous. We have the opportunity to open to a limitless possibility, to transform our mundane awareness into Divine awareness. But even though Divinity is always available to us, it's not that we simply contact It and immediately feel blissed out and full of light. We have to continually tune in to God. It's like dialing in a radio station. It takes a while to develop our ability to get strong, clear reception.

However, if we don't make the choice to refine our inner dial at this very moment, and continue to choose it every moment— even when we don't feel the clarity—there will never be a time when we find what's within us. It takes real consciousness and real effort and discipline to keep dialing away from the things that make us so miserable but, oddly enough, comfortable at the same time.

BEING GRATEFUL FOR THE OPPORTUNITY TO CHOOSE

The choice to live a spiritual life is cause for celebration. It's incredible that we have been given the Grace of choosing spirituality in this lifetime. Just walk down any street, anywhere on this planet, pay attention and you will see that most people are not even aware of this choice. We cannot be arrogant about it. We have to be grateful. It is irrelevant how and why any of us have come to have the opportunity to grow spiritually. The issue is whether we choose to take advantage of that opportunity.

The reality is that there is probably not a person reading this book who faces the real challenges of survival encountered by most people on the face of the earth today. We think we have hard lives, but we don't have a clue about what others must endure. Travel to any troubled spot on the globe, or even just drive a few miles to the closest inner city, and you will witness the difficulty most people live in. The point is that we don't have to face that kind of fight for mere survival. Our dramas center around how many millions of dollars we are going to make, or not make—and whether we can be fulfilled if we don't have that kind of money. We are ignorant about real hardship, yet we build all these dramas around our everyday activities.

This is not to say we don't face real obstacles in our lives—but the reality is that our problems are never as massive as we believe them to be. It is our mind, our ego, and our drama that blow everything out of proportion. We have all had the experience of choosing to open our heart in a moment of crisis; choosing to go beyond the contraction and by so doing, having a mountainous obstacle disappear. What is it that changes the chemistry of what we encounter? We learn to use subtle discrimination to find a simple place in ourselves and we learn to live from an open heart on a permanent basis. Then it doesn't make a difference how big the mountain is or how hard it might be to work through it.

Rudi described it this way: If you take a mouse and drop it into a bag of flour, the mouse thinks "lunch" and starts eating its way out. If you take a person and drop him into a similar situation, he will get hysterical and freeze up. The mind says, "I don't know what to do," and it starts creating drama. It requires consciousness to recognize the actual difficulty of a situation and not mentally inflate the problem. This is not to deny that something is hard, but to recognize that there is a place from which we must approach life in order to transform our ability to respond.

We can only find this inner resource by opening our heart and feeling the flow. This is how we begin to internalize the challenging situations in our life. It is how we develop the flow between inner and outer. We slowly eat our way out of the bag.

We may lose a few teeth in the process of chewing on it, but we simply keep chewing. Then the obstacle becomes nourishment instead of suffocation.

OVERCOMING FEAR

So many times we find ourselves faced with the choice of living in fear or becoming fearless. One of the problems with fear is that it tends to set up a vicious cycle. We immediately reinforce its reality by thinking, "I did something wrong: I am bad," or by analyzing what it is in us that attracts fearful situations. Ultimately, we must take control, because whatever we feed will get stronger in us. We can imagine our fear being like a dog. We can invite it to come out and play, but at some point it's time to exert our authority and say, "Go lie down." The power to create our own life is what determines our experience. We have to accept the responsibility that if we choose fear, we are using our power to choose fear.

As soon as I met Rudi, I learned a very valuable lesson about fear. I had been so incredibly afraid of my father that I never once opened my heart to him. From my perspective he was the toughest man on the face of the earth. The day I met Rudi my relationship with my father changed. It was amazing. My father didn't change a bit, but something in me was able to change how I related to him. It was a powerful experience for me, and it is the same experience that plays out in everyone's lives.

The things we fear are camouflages. They are not real. We attach our fears to something distinct, and that is how we keep them alive and give them validity. But as soon as we disconnect fear from a dynamic or a person, we recognize it for what it is— some internal vibration that has essentially nothing to do with the apparition it creates out there in front of us. A conscious person says, "What is this, where did this come from? What is it in me that is afraid?" And we can then inspect it, but in the sense of tuning in to the source of the fear rather than analyzing the particulars.

STRONGER THAN EMOTIONS AND FREER THAN MIND

Part of growing is choosing not to live in our emotions. When they come up, we often wallow in them and drown. Our emotions are a fundamental part of our human condition, but we do not have to live there. When we are locked in emotion we are contracted and there is no flow. So we find a different approach—one of not reacting, not getting caught in the drama of the situation or the personal injustice we encountered. Instead, we quickly learn that life doesn't have to affect us in this way.

We create problems for ourselves because we categorize. We believe, "This shouldn't have happened . . . it should have been *this,*" instead of recognizing that whatever *did* happen is simply strong energy. And we can either send any powerful energy to our mind or we can draw it into our heart and into the flow, and burn it. The fundamental decision to keep our energy inside results in a new ability to respond more appropriately. The mind isn't negative, but it has a limited capacity to perceive. It functions within a certain band of resonance. The mind only becomes a problem when it causes contraction, when it stops the flow.

The mind is not the same as intellect. Focusing on keeping our awareness in our heart does not prohibit us from engaging in mental activity at the same time, nor do we have to live alone in a cave in order to do spiritual work. It's our limited understanding that says, "No, I can't live in the full presence of Oneness, my heart exploding with radiance, while I'm solving math problems and dealing with an emotional struggle with my partner."

When we find ourselves limiting our options in this way, the first thing we must do is get out of our head and tune in and open our heart. Then most of the tension will dissolve. Too often, the first thing we actually do is stop breathing, stop opening, and start projecting onto somebody else. Or, we try to change some situation that wasn't what we wanted or expected. When we begin to see all our hardships and pain as nourishment rather than difficulty and drama, we have a completely different relationship to the people and situations we encounter in our life. Then we are not trying to change anything except ourselves, and where we live in ourselves. This is a very subtle but important shift in awareness.

RECOGNIZING AND TRANSCENDING OUR PATTERNS

The reason we must bring so much discipline to our spiritual practice is that when we make the choice to grow, every limitation within us begins to show up — right in our face! *Kuṇḍalinī* has the power to first uncover and then dissolve obstacles in our psychic system, and this means not only the contractions, tensions, and patterns of this lifetime, but the accumulated karma of innumerable lifetimes. We must consciously choose to free ourselves of *every* limitation, especially those that lie hidden, waiting for us to become strong enough to expose and overcome them.

As we work to deepen ourselves spiritually we begin to see patterns that have been ground into a groove, through the continuous repetition of investing our life force in the same place. Our patterns are what keep us trapped in lifetime after lifetime of suffering. As we grow and become quieter in ourselves, we are able to not only see our patterns coming but to sidestep them. If we are not quiet enough, what happens is that we are suddenly caught in turmoil. The reaction is, "How did I get *here*?" At that moment, all we can do is recognize the pattern and lift ourselves above it.

As long as we have allowed a pattern to engage and catch our life force, that pattern will repeat itself endlessly. Every time it comes around it looks different, but it is actually the same. The people are different, the dynamics are different, but it is the same pattern and it is ours. Whatever the pattern is — whether it is one of self-rejection or arrogance — it reinforces the ego. The thinnest veils of our ego are wrapped inside our deepest patterns. The good news is that as we grow, we automatically expose them. This *is* good news, because we cannot change a pattern unless we are conscious of it. Our patterns interconnect with those of the people around us. This is what binds us to these people, and why they are present in our lives.

So what do we do about patterns? Recognize and transcend them. Recognize that whatever arises is *our* pattern and *our* dynamic. If we truly want to be transformed, we must find and live from a different place inside that does not reinforce our patterns. The problem is that we generally do not see the levels where we are trapped, and spiritual growth does not happen without consciousness. If we were aware of our patterns of behavior we would change them. Who would consciously choose to suffer?

When we do recognize our deep limitations and patterns, it's rather hard to take. Witnessing the things we keep doing— to ourselves and to the people we interact with—makes us uncomfortable, because we have exposed the parts of ourselves that we find intolerable. But whether we know it or not, when our patterns are uncovered some deeper part of us is asking for them to be revealed. Real suffering comes from being separated from our own Divine Source. Compared to that, the pain of exposing our patterns is minimal. This dimension of pain is only significant when we lack a broader perspective—when we cannot see past the dynamics of what is happening. When we remain in our center, our discomfort is experienced as part of the extraordinary joy of the possibility of living in openness and freedom.

Patterns are created by the repetition of investing our life force in our worldly existence, and we must burn and transform them if we want to free that energy to rise back up to God. We redirect the energy from the horizontal dimension—going around and around because it has nowhere else to go—and project it vertically. Then, in that higher dimension, we find another repetition of pattern, and again we free ourselves from that trap and, like rocket fuel, we use that energy to move up. We do not have to go looking for our patterns, because they will be revealed to us in the process of growing.

FROM PATTERNS EMERGE OUR CONTRACTIONS

Contractions emerge from our deepest patterns and also represent our inability to stay open to the ever-flowing changes in life. Contractions happen when we are so caught in a situation that we squeeze the very life force out of the change that is trying to take place, prohibiting any real growth. The only solution is to employ the same technique we use in dealing with patterns—we put the energy of the contraction back into the flow and burn it. When that energy is inside us, it is not outside re-creating and feeding the pattern. It is important to be very quiet and still, and find a flow inside when we are digesting this energy.

We are not growing and changing if we are continually reactive and spewing out negativity. Behaving this way directs our energy externally and does not allow us to invest that force in our growth. And of course, we have to be aware of how we affect the people around us. We should always go back inside to find a state of openness, even in the midst of our own contraction.

From that openness and flow we can do the work of transmuting the energy of the contraction—and although we may not always be cheerful, we will not be expressing our tension outwardly. Keeping our awareness inside and dealing with our tensions requires work, and as we burn through our internal density we will feel the heat of that transformation. Don't be surprised if you run a "psychic temperature" on a regular basis!

Regardless of whether we are working on our patterns, contractions, resistance, tensions, or karma, we must not approach any of it from our mind or emotions. If we want to transcend our limitations, we must function from within God's heart, which is of course found in each of us. From there we engage in the process of transformation, instead of fighting against the very thing that has shown up in our life to enable us to grow. We can celebrate our own contraction and the potential for freedom it reveals to us, so that even when we are in the midst of some struggle, there is still openness within us. When we do this, we are able to avoid bludgeoning the people around us with the pressure we feel.

Above all, we must not take our own patterns, contractions, resistance, and tensions personally. How do we do that? It is both profoundly simple and yet really hard to do. We must become bigger than these limitations so that we are not buried inside them. When we realize that every challenge in our life emerges precisely to free the Divine within us, that knowledge changes everything. Whether it takes a day, a month, or a year, we deal with everything from this perspective and from a state of openness. We allow a contraction to burn up because we are detached from it being about us, or at least from the limited egoic "us" that we identify as ourselves. When we are bigger than the contraction, its energy is in the flow and it is being processed.

BURNING THE KARMA FROM PAST LIFETIMES

As we burn through the obstacles to our spiritual freedom, we realize that we are not only dealing with our current tensions, patterns, and contractions, but also those we have brought into this life from other lifetimes. There is extraordinary inertia stored within our psychic body, and it takes amazing power to free ourselves from this residue. If we get caught in the particulars of a contraction, we are missing the point. We think, "I did something, or somebody else did something, and now I am contracted," but the truth is that any dynamic is simply the current manifestation of our ongoing karma.

The deepest pattern, and the one we most need to break, is that we contract when it is time to open. Seen from this point of view, the specifics of any contraction are irrelevant. We do not have to know what the pattern was, what it is called, or who was part of its history. What we really need to be free of is the pattern of contraction itself. We always want to fabricate some content around every contraction. We then create a lot of drama about the content and get lost in our mind and emotions, rather than looking inside and overcoming the propensity to close.

If the contraction is big, the openness and flow must be bigger. Anchored in stillness, in a state of consciousness and surrender, we allow ourselves to be freed of whatever has manifested. We rise above limitation by consciously processing it. Although it may be hard work to do this, there will be a time when we actually feel elation whenever we have exposed our own limitation. We can feel the contraction and yet we do not close down—and we are not tempted to run off and escape. We realize that we have been given the chance to change. Seeing what kind of a jerk you are is a good thing—and even when we didn't want to know, we receive the gift of seeing it!

The biggest opportunities for change are the ones we do not ask for, because we would never ask for them. If you want to be coddled, do not do spiritual work. The density of our own ego is almost a match for the extraordinary power of the Divinity within us, and in the process of breaking the ego's grip all of our faults will be exposed.

If we are not prepared to see our own dirty laundry and that of the people around us, we are not going to grow. Padmasambhava said, "True faith and surrender is forged in the fire of challenging times." We must face the grip of our ego and face the fact that our limited experience in life is the direct result of continually reinforcing that ego, lifetime after lifetime.

RESISTANCE IS THE UNWILLINGNESS TO GROW

We go through big contractions on a regular basis, and my advice is to go through them with consciousness. Go through them knowing the power of the change inherent within the contraction, the power of the change that is available within you. Resistance is the unwillingness to grow and change when our life asks us to do so. When we feel resistance, one of two things might be happening—we are either growing, or we are not growing. If we are growing, we are going to feel our resistance because we are exposing deeper levels of limitation within. This exposure threatens our ego, which takes a stand against changing the status quo, and we feel the pressure. On the other hand, if we are not growing, our resistance will be expressed all over the place. And when we do not open and get past the resistance, its energy goes back into the pattern, enlarging and strengthening it.

We have not really changed anything until we have completely let go of everything that was part of a pattern. The last moment of release requires as much energy as whatever brought us to that pattern, and if we wish to push through all our resistance, we must take refuge in our own heart and in God's heart. If we cannot find real inner depth in these moments, my own personal experience is that change will not occur. I have never been able to change without going back to my heart and surrendering into it. When we surrender into our heart we enlarge the openness, because we feed it with the very energy that created the struggle.

I've said that enlightenment happens in a moment, and then it takes a lifetime to actuate it. It doesn't really make a difference whether enlightenment comes first and then we integrate it, or we first do the inner work of opening that allows enlightenment to become our permanent experience. It also does not matter what we are caught in that keeps us from our own realization. What does it matter whether it's a small entanglement, such as one little knot in a strand of yarn, or thousands of knots in the yarn? God never gives us more than we can handle. The size of whatever we need to face sometimes looks a lot bigger than we think we can deal with—and this is the very thing we *must* deal with.

The Need to Become Bigger

We must rise to the level of energy that life in the world demands of us. The conscious person does not say, "I just can't deal with that, and I'm going to contract because of it." The life that has been given to us provides the nourishment and energy we need to grow bigger inside. As I have discussed, inner and outer cannot be separated. When we think our life is demanding too much of us, the conscious person says, "No. This demand is there for a reason. I must become bigger." We meet that demand and pull the energy out of it, bringing it inside. We cultivate a bigger openness, and then we extend that expanded energy back out into the situation at hand.

Getting bigger means expanding past the constricting boundaries we encounter within ourselves. The process of purification and transformation will burn up blocks in our system, but we must do our work from a state of openness. What we are trying to do is integrate body and Spirit, and that happens through consciousness.

Transcending the duality of life is about integrating the spiritual and material worlds, and recognizing that they are not different, but simply diversified waves of the same energy field. This understanding comes from our own awareness, which we contact within and then extend outwardly. We are never separate from our consciousness.

The real pain in our lives does not come from the trials of everyday living. It stems from the fundamental pain of being separate from God. The reward is instant when we tether ourselves to Divinity. We say, "I wish to grow and I want to know God." The catch is that we cannot then negotiate any point after making this statement. We do not get to dictate the exact course of our lives—only how we live within the course of that life.

Sometimes we have to choose to do things or to engage in the world in ways that are difficult. But we come to realize that these situations have been chosen for us for a reason, because we need to build some strength. Living an extraordinary life is coming to understand that principle. We choose to live the life God has given us with profound joy, gratitude, and depth.

If we cannot find freedom in our current life, we will never find it in some other life, and we will certainly never ever find it in somebody else's life. That does not mean we do not have relationships and celebrate in the joy of sharing our lives with others. But what we want to do is find that place in our heart wherein we make the highest choices for our own life, as it has been given to us. What a truly amazing accomplishment that would be!

WHAT REALLY NEEDS TO CHANGE

The things we have in our life that we think we need to change have manifested expressly to change us. These dynamics may never change at all. Nothing changes in our life if we do not change inside. We can have a different house. We can change our partner. We can change this or that, but we have not really changed anything. We are still on the same merry-go-round. We can only get bigger by accepting the way things are and opening around those circumstances or patterns.

Control is always the fallback position of the ego. If life is not going the way we want it, we think we will figure out how to manipulate it. We spend our lives trying to control something we cannot control, and do not need to control in the first place.

When we find ourselves in a demanding situation that affords a real chance to transform our consciousness—to understand life from a completely different place—we have to abandon the logic and the rationale that brought us there, at that moment. In doing so, there is profound joy because we see the possibility of change through accepting what is and giving up control.

Living within ourselves and accepting the life we have been given takes profound trust. First, we have to trust ourselves, because that is the basis for trusting God. We learn to tune in to the part of us that is free and lives in joy. We tune in, and we stay tuned in, no matter what we are engaged in doing. When we trust enough to surrender control, everything can change.

This process is not a giving up or a giving in. At some point we see that life as we have known it is like a broken record. The same thing keeps repeating itself again and again, and we understand that we remain stuck because we are continually bringing the same level of consciousness to our life. It is exactly when we find ourselves spinning in circles that we have to find a totally new person inside, in a place filled with God. The ego will not change itself. When we understand this, the realization itself comes from the same vital force within that is trying to free us.

I've said that to get beyond our limitations, we must burn them in the fire of transformation. In this process, what we experience is that we ourselves are being "cooked." Know that being transformed requires that we not only have the courage and the openness to watch this happen, but also the profound longing to stoke the fire. We often get to the point where we say, "Well, I don't have to cook my soup anymore. I'm done." The catch is that you are not the chef. A consciousness much greater than our own is doing the cooking!

If we do not do this work, what happens to our life force as our patterns, contractions, resistance, and tensions merge into each other? This energy gets stuck inside and squeezes the life force out of us, compressing our openness, energy, and consciousness. This is the density that encases Spirit, and which restricts our life. If we live in our density, in this soup pot of all our negativity, what manifests for us?

We try to have an outlet for all this pain, compression, tension, and pattern—and generally this means reaching out and doing something to somebody else. In this state of pain and confusion we are not concerned with freeing ourselves. We are simply trying to relieve the pain at whatever cost, and so we generate karma, the inevitable result of our self-serving actions.

What happens with this matrix of suppression, tension, patterns, and karma that we have been producing is that we take it with us, in the form of blocks and knots in our psychic system called *granthi*. They are balls of tension and trauma accumulated over lifetimes, and these *granthi* are carried within our subtle body from one lifetime to the next. In order to dissolve the *granthi*, we have to create some openness instead of reinforcing the knots. The way to begin to get some movement inside of the density is to cultivate flow, because flow is energy in motion.

STAYING FOCUSED ON TRANSFORMATION

In order to get past all of our limitations, our work must be to free the Divinity within us, allowing It to express Itself as our life. This transformation is in a completely different dimension from changing our behavior or personality. It requires an indescribably profound change in consciousness, and because we literally cannot imagine this level of freedom, we often have trouble staying focused on it.

The reason spiritual growth takes so long is that we get so caught up in today's drama and tension, or what someone did to us yesterday, and what we are going to do to them tomorrow.

We get trapped in all of this turmoil, and therefore we end up creating more tension instead of burning it and freeing ourselves.

Through the Grace of the Divine, when *Kuṇḍalinī* knocks on your door and it is time to wake up, recognize that you are no longer in control. She is. That vital force is going to awaken in us. But it is our resistance to the very thing that God is trying to give us—which manifests as our life—which keeps awakening from happening. This resistance shows itself in the tensions and dramas we create, and the mundane things we get involved with. The coalescence of all that misuse of our own life force creates the *granthi* that do not allow the Divinity to rise up within us. *Kuṇḍalinī sādhana* is, on one hand, the completely technical process of learning how to get free, and it is also the unconditional surrender to that process.

Sometimes, in the midst of transformation, we run into major turbulence, and when this occurs we need to be especially vigilant about staying open to whatever change is trying to manifest. If we cannot manage our energy at this point, we can feel as if we are in the midst of a huge explosion and life seems chaotic. This happens when we are up against a knot and the energy is trying to release the blockage—but because we cannot stay internalized, that force gets projected outward.

When the energy erupts, we might get angry or start blaming ourselves, or we forget to focus on just the energy itself and therefore project content where none exists. If we do this, we just wrap another knot around the tangle of yarn. That is why we must not take it personally when our tensions are exposed. We have to recognize the pattern and be aware that knotted-up energy is now trying to unwind.

Difficult situations require us to go deeper into ourselves and find a place that we have never discovered before. But ironically, the deeper we go inside, the more challenge we will experience in terms of something threatening to pull us out of our center. We are exposing more entrenched patterns, and must therefore find the resources to transmute that intense energy.

We go through the discipline of practicing every day so that when those difficult situations do come, we have developed the inner mechanism to deal with them. The preparation is our daily work and we must be ready to face anything and any degree of difficulty. But if we do not have unwavering commitment—if we are not prepared to do whatever it takes to internalize the energy of any experience, no matter what comes along—perhaps all the training in the world will not help us.

GROWING IS NOT FOR OSTRICHES

When we find some new place in ourselves, we go back into the world and hope that we can bring a deeper awareness to it. But sometimes we fall flat on our face. The worst thing to do is to start beating ourselves up over our failure. All this would accomplish is the continuation of our current contraction. It's better to move on and try to be bigger and open our heart more when that same type of situation presents itself again. This is why we use the term spiritual "practice" and why Rudi called it "work." It requires work to find a new dimension in ourselves and then integrate our inner experience into every aspect of our lives.

Rudi named his book *Spiritual Cannibalism* because this expresses the process of growing and freeing ourselves from ourselves. His directive for spiritual practitioners was, "Life must be consumed whole, with all its pain, joy, and sorrow." How wonderful that we have this opportunity to expand beyond our limited boundaries by absorbing the energy of every experience.

We talk about the wish to grow, how our wish matures into commitment, and ultimately how that commitment becomes surrender. What we surrender to is an understanding that every pressure is exactly what we need in our life to find a deeper opening—it is what we need in order to continue our own work. Surrender is both the letting go of our perspective and a profound acceptance of whatever life offers us.

Throughout the process of assimilating the energy from our experiences, we have to avoid turning into a ball of knots inside by engaging in mental gymnastics. We can easily get lost in trying to sort out the origin of our current dilemma. We think, "My mother didn't give me anything I wanted, and that is why I am a wreck." Or, "It was probably something from my last lifetime." This kind of thinking is nonsense. It is right here, right now, that we engage with the bag of cement we just had to swallow. Are we going to digest it, or are we going to attach some drama to it in a futile attempt to figure out why it is there in the first place? We need to stay focused and consciously deal with whatever is right in our face at the moment.

Growing in this way is not easy. Left to our own devices, we would remain a small person with a heart the size of a matchbox. It is only Life itself, and the Divinity which has given us life, that provides us the conditions we need to grow. We become bigger by consciously accepting what is given, and always being grateful for the power, fuel, and nourishment provided for us—knowing that we cannot negotiate what this fuel looks like. If we reject the difficult things in our life, we become spiritual ostriches, sticking our heads in the ground. We foolishly believe that if we do not deal with our difficulties, they won't limit us.

If we compare spiritual growth to athletics, all the training in the world will not necessarily mean that we win the game if we lose our focus and awareness. We must have the inner fire, and yet motivation is not enough. I have mentioned Kabir's beautiful poem in which he says that it is the intensity of the longing that does all the work. While this is true, conscious choice and disciplined action are also required, because we have to prove in ourselves, to ourselves, and to the God within every day, that what we say we want is indeed what we want. Talk is cheap. And it's a waste of time when we avoid making a real commitment to growth, when our real feeling is, "I want to be free, but I just don't want to have to pay for it." So we deepen our commitment and focus, and accept whatever situation is presented to us. We think in terms of the result, not about how much work we have to do. All we have to really do is give up our tensions!

FREE WILL AND COMMITMENT

We have to remember that having the free will to choose and to focus on growing does not mean we can control every aspect of our lives. Some things we do not get to choose. Our free will is expressed in terms of how we live within what is given to us, and most importantly, by deciding where we project the energy of our life—into the world, or back into ourselves.

The greatest act of our own free will is to surrender it. At the end of the Bhagavad Gita, it says, "Thy will, not my will." We all have the choice to surrender, but *when* we decide to make that choice is a critical point in our growth. Make it early, or make it late. We make it not because we are forced to, but because we celebrate the opportunity to give our life back to God—and that is the highest expression of free will. It is only in the state of freedom in God that complete happiness is permanent. The only way we can honor the gifts we receive in this life is to grow, and it is by opening our heart that we find the extraordinary life within us. Our wish opens the door and our commitment allows us to walk through it.

In my youth I was an atheist. All of a sudden, one day all I could do was think about God. Three days later, I heard about Rudi and then I went through a circuitous route of meeting him. I consider myself profoundly lucky that I listened to the powerful impulse of life within me, which led me to find my teacher. Even if it is a very faint voice, tune in to the place it comes from; then nourish and feed that connection. An innate knowing is within all of us, and that is why we suddenly find ourselves with a real opportunity for spiritual growth, even when we were not consciously looking for it. When Grace is offered, we had better take it because it may not be granted again any time soon. And when the gift is given, listen very carefully to the message it contains.

Choosing to Stay in Our Spiritual Practice

It is important that each of us realizes that not many people truly make the conscious choice to find God, to live in service of God, and live an extraordinary life. From my perspective, there is only one reason to choose it—because we want to live in the heart of God, and we want to be happy, no matter what.

It really does not make a difference why we come to a spiritual practice. The only thing that matters is why we stay. We need to get beyond needing quick, superficial doses of happiness. Not only does this type of fulfillment not last, but there is also a profound distinction between being happy in the moment and the deep joy that comes from opening our heart and feeling God inside. Opening to this deeper resonance is the all-important conscious choice we all must make. And although change and transformation are not without some pain, let us really be honest with ourselves. When we were not trying to grow and change, were we without pain then?

It is my personal experience and belief, after having watched many people come and go in spiritual practice, that if we do not make and hold on to an unshakable commitment to grow, something will distract us. We all get tested. We forget our commitment whenever the very force we have activated within us puts obstacles in front of us that will provide the chance to actually grow. The commitment is the vow to live in God's heart instead of in our small self. By transcending duality, we allow this higher Consciousness to express Itself through us. If we are centered, and are living from that awareness, we cannot get lost. We are so deeply established in our commitment that there are no other options but to remain on course. Discipline is our devotion in action, and if we truly love God and truly want to be happy, then work and discipline are a joy.

If we do not make the conscious choice moment by moment to live a deeply spiritual life, we certainly cannot suddenly arrive at the end of our life having achieved what we said we wanted. We must be centered and consciously engage our lives with disciplined action. Eventually, an authentic spiritual person will have worked so deeply and long enough that nothing of them remains. Only God exists. We recognize and experience the total unity of life—and that is the test, the glory, and the celebration of our existence.

SURRENDER:
THE DOORWAY INTO THE DIVINE

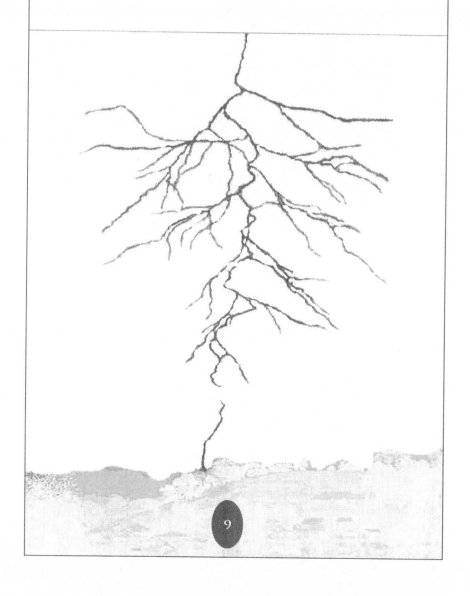

9

CHAPTER NINE

Imagine there are two doors in front of you. Door number one is marked "The Door of Surrender" and the other is "My Life by My Design." Beyond the door of surrender is your life, unfolding through and in the Grace of the Divine. Behind the other door is your life, unfolding as you would design it based on your preferences, understanding, and concepts. Which door would you choose? Probably we all would say, "Of course I would choose door number one." Yet the dilemma lies in the fact that although we want to know and live in the heart of God, we are also bound by the fear of not knowing what awaits us on the other side of the door of surrender.

We might think, "I'm not quite that advanced yet, to reach into unconditional surrender." The point is we never will be, unless we practice. There is not one moment of surrender; there is every moment of surrender. We can only surrender now. We can't surrender later. All too often we believe that the conditions of our life have to be ideal before we can surrender. We are hoping that life is going to be different, and therefore we won't have to change. Surrender is both something we practice and ultimately a state we live in. The state of surrender is the experience of Oneness and unconditional trust in the Divine.

The inner work is one of letting go completely, until we have the intimate experience of Oneness. The outer work is the expression of that experience through the trusting and accepting of a higher force working within us and in our life. Everything we do in our spiritual practice is cultivating the ground, bringing us to a state of surrender. There is a beautiful saying, "The Grace of the Divine cannot descend into us until our surrender ascends to God."

TRUSTING GOD

We practice surrender until we do not need to anymore, because it has become our permanent state. Even if you only glimpse that state for five seconds, it will make you a servant for life. Rudi's final words, dictated moments before his plane crashed, put this into perspective. His words are worth repeating:

> *The last year of my life has prepared me for the understanding that Divine Consciousness can come only through unconditional surrender into our own nothingness. That state is reached by surrendering ourselves and the tensions that bind, restrict, and keep us from expressing the power of that creation that is our own true essence. It is God flowing through us, and showing us that we are nothing but Him. I want to live as an expression of that higher creative will, and from a deeper sense of surrender.*

Rudi was an extraordinary person who worked very hard in his life, but even with his last breath, surrendering to God was foremost in his mind.

The problem for most of us is that we allow everything else to interfere with our surrender. Saint Ignatius, founder of the Jesuits, said the following, "There are very few men who realize what God would make of them if they abandoned themselves entirely to His hands, and let themselves be formed by His Grace. A thick and shapeless tree trunk would never believe that it could become a statue, admired as a miracle of sculpture . . . and would never consent to submit itself to the chisel of the sculptor who, as Saint Augustine says, sees by his genius what he can make of it."

Surrender is the ultimate trust in God. It is amazing that we cannot allow ourselves to trust the same power that holds galaxies together to also handle our little lives. And what's worse, we somehow have the arrogance to believe we can manage better on our own. Why are we so afraid of surrendering to God? What is it that we are really surrendering? Control, fears, illusions, individuality—you know . . . our ego. But why wouldn't we want to surrender our attachments and limitations? They are what keep us bound and unable to recognize our own Divine Consciousness.

The ego is a trickster and it has the incredible capacity to camouflage every one of our attachments—to make us believe that without these limitations we would have no identity. But it is precisely by letting go of these inner restrictions that we discover our true Self. We must be prepared to surrender what we think we most need in our lives, and not just lay down whatever we already feel we do not need. And it's important to remember that nonattachment does not mean "not having" but rather "not holding."

Real surrender means not holding on to the things we so firmly believe we must have to make life whole. If our goal is freedom, we place our attention on gaining it. We hold on to that goal. Then, as life presents things that restrict our growth, it is a simple choice to let go of them.

Most people think surrendering is an act of weakness, but it is actually the inability to surrender that reflects a lack of strength. The whole discussion of surrender to God boils down to one thing—the fear that we might have to give up our individual will. Why not focus on the love and Grace that is available by moving beyond our limitations? True surrender is unconditional, and it is the key to liberation.

WE FOCUS ON GOD, NOT ON OUR FEAR

Surrender is an inner experience and an outer expression of trust. How do we learn trust if we do not practice it? Rudi described surrender as voluntarily casting off all thoughts and emotions that inhibit our access to our own Spirit. An open heart, humility, and courage are qualities we must cultivate in order to surrender. It is in our open heart that we experience God, and it is only to God that we surrender. If we really open our heart and feel God, then surrender is a non-issue.

Humility is one of the traits that enable us to move beyond our limited perspective and open to God. Isn't it interesting that we can go to the Grand Canyon and stand there in awe? Likewise, we can look at the vast night sky, see the endless galaxies, and be filled with amazement and wonder. Experiences like that help us find some humility, some sense of how small we are. Yet the Source of all of this greatness and majesty is infinitely more profound than the manifest universe. The paradox of life is that we come to realize we are at once a speck and, at the same time, the entire infinite. In fact, spiritual growth could be described as becoming that infinite, instead of remaining the speck.

Let us focus on the infinite. The ego is convinced that it is separate from that greatness, and this misunderstanding is what keeps us finite. Within every one of us there is a voice that says, "I want to know God," but very few people will say, "I want to know God and I don't care what the costs are." We think we know what is beyond the door labeled "My Life by My Design," but we hesitate to enter "The Door of Surrender" because we fear giving up control. Each of us must find a place of unconditional trust within, because this is the foundation of surrender. If it is our intention to grow, then the highest use of our individual will is to surrender it and align ourselves with Divine Will. We do have free will. We choose what we want in this life. Think very carefully about how much you really want to know God.

Why are we so afraid of changing? What is our deepest fear? On the way to our realization, we undergo a process that can be described as dying without dying. We change so radically that our identity as a separate individual is dissolved. In this sense you could say we die, but when we pass beyond dying what we find is rebirth. The term *saṃnyāsa* means "twice born," which is the same language used in Christianity and in many other cultures and traditions. *Jīvanmukti*, which means freedom in this lifetime, is the Sanskrit expression of this transformation. Those who have attained this state of freedom know that giving up one's separate identity is feared only as long as an individual is locked in isolation. Once separation is surrendered, there is only Unity.

Until we get past our personal anxiety about death, and about losing our identity, what can we do? Opening our heart is a good place to start, because if we can't open, we can't do what we need to do, which is surrender. And although the dissolution of the ego brings us our realization, having an open heart is a prerequisite for liberation. Certainly if we cannot open our heart, then we must intensify our conscious effort to break down the thickness and resistance in us. We must dissolve any obstacles that block us from opening to the vital force within.

Surrender is not a matter of doing. It's really a process of undoing. The depth of surrender can be tested by what we do in life, but the act of surrender is always a matter of dissolving limitation and contraction. We are undoing the bindings that constrict us and the hold the ego has on us. However, transformation does not happen by beating up the ego or by attending weekly self-help workshops, but by going inside and letting go. Then our life in the world becomes the outer expression of our inner work. You cannot separate the two. Life is both the test and the proof of that internal experience.

Surrender is learning, undoing, and stripping away our misunderstanding—and our willingness to allow that to happen will be tested. Everything in the world is a test of how profoundly we want to hold on to the experience of Oneness within ourselves. Anything that takes us out of that state of Oneness has to be surrendered. And if something truly takes us into Oneness, hold on to that and celebrate it.

PERMANENT CHANGE MEANS CONTINUED WORK

When we open our heart, we change our consciousness. That is why we surrender. We may have a fleeting glimpse of the potential for transformation in a moment of real openness. We see the light in everything and we are profoundly surrendered. But did that moment of surrender permanently transform us? Potentially it could—but if it did not, we had better keep opening our heart and doing our inner work in order to have that experience repeatedly.

We often hear of people who have had some profound experience. They feel it. They know it and yet, somehow, they lose the awareness. Quite often it is the silt, the residue of daily living that covers up the light. The light never went off. It is always on. But we need God's help to perceive it, and so we meditate, open our heart, and then work to extend that inner experience out into our world.

I am fairly pragmatic and my message is not all love and bliss, because we have to recognize that there is a lot of hard work that must be done to break through our barriers. If any individual could simply sit down, completely let go, and open their heart, then there would be nothing else to do. We are searching for bliss, yet somehow we forget that having it is up to us.

The continued process of letting go can only happen in the heart. If we do not surrender at every moment, the ego will co-opt the power we have found within ourselves, and our openness will dissipate. This is why we may experience a breakthrough but then lose it. Every single one of us, no matter how deeply we live in a state of surrender, will, if we are truly growing, always face a deeper need to surrender—until there is no individual, no ego remaining and we are in a state of Oneness. Then, realization is not just something we have read about, had a glimpse of, or heard a teacher describe. We have experienced it, and we have allowed that experience to grow. This is how we surrender all limitation and permanently transform our consciousness.

WHAT WE ARE SURRENDERING

Surrender is different from stress management. It is not a matter of being unattached to the small, upsetting things in everyday life. We can become more relaxed on this level, but this is not the depth of surrender that's required for spiritual growth. The real work is internal, and what we have to eventually give up includes who we know ourselves to be, who we see ourselves as, and what we identify with. It's harder to let go of these internal limitations because they are central to our understanding of who we think we are. It takes true courage to walk through the door of surrender and give up our self-image. Even when we are not completely clear that we have to work on such a fundamental level, we still have to let go of our identity because it is that very image that creates our inner dialogue, our hesitation about surrendering more deeply.

Rudi said, "To surrender is to surrender completely. Not just what you wish to surrender, or think needs to be surrendered, but a total letting go." While that sounds like a platitude, it is a very practical description of the work we do. We must bring this understanding to the daily reality of letting go, while seeking to surrender on a deeper level.

Often it is hard to know whether pursuing our goals is legitimate or an expression of our willfulness—an expression of our inability to surrender to what is really being asked of us. It takes true discrimination to discern the difference, and mostly, it requires the ability to feel the energetic support of what we are trying to accomplish. If the energetic support is there, then things happen. There is crystal clarity in our intention, and apparent obstacles fall away. If that support is not present, we can often force something to happen, but it probably is not what is really needed in our lives.

Part of surrender is accepting, waiting, and having the patience to open inside. Working in this way, we find the understanding that if something is needed in life, it will come. It requires subtle discernment to ask repeatedly whenever a situation is unclear. My personal experience is that it does become clear whether our desire is originating from our will or ego, or from a higher place within ourselves. The problem is that we do not ask—or if we do, we grab hold of the first answer we receive. We are usually impatient and do not ask with enough depth, so the answer is not coming from higher consciousness. That is why we must learn to really open, wait, listen, ask, and use subtle discrimination. Without making this profound inner contact and having even a fleeting glimpse of our own Oneness, I do not think one can surrender. Without this degree of contact, we are just negotiating with God. And that is a mental process, not an offering of oneself from the heart.

Rudi said to his students, "We have nothing in us that can truly understand the infinite capacity for growth available to every human being. It isn't until we pass through the doorway of complete surrender that we really have a sense of the fulfillment available to us. Your work is to find a deep wish, and a profound inner surrender."

BUILDING A SOLID FOUNDATION FOR CHANGE

We do not know what surrender is until we do it. Why would we want to negotiate with the life that is trying to unfold for us? Living an extraordinary life means celebrating what has been given to us, instead of pining for the life we are always trying to fabricate. If we really are quiet and use our inner discrimination, we will know whether we are building something on quicksand or if it has a solid foundation. We can use force to hammer away and create a beautiful structure, but it will be unsupported unless the impetus for creation comes from that quiet place within.

If we are focused on growing instead of being attached to a specific outcome, then we ask ourselves, "Do I need this to grow?" If we seek guidance about the choices in our lives based on that question, we will receive a reliable answer, because we are asking from a deeper part of ourselves. We are connecting to a higher consciousness and letting that inform us. When we are not in touch with our Self, we can be sure that our decisions can only come from our limited understanding.

When ice melts, it takes as much energy to raise the temperature that last degree—to the point where the ice will totally dissolve into water—as it does to reach one degree below that point. The Divine is pure, unbounded awareness and it exists within us. But we are all attached to our thickness to a greater or lesser extent, so there are layers of barriers we must transcend if we want to experience our Divinity. We must continually surrender the thickness that keeps us from getting in contact with the simple state of Oneness. This is the work and the practice, and we sometimes do not get it exactly right. That is okay.

We have to dig deeper in ourselves to find the unshakable conviction that our mind and emotions, which are the instruments of the ego, are, in fact, limited. The manifestations of encountering our limited self will look different, feel different, and have a different face, a different name, and a different dynamic every time—until we pull back and see that this is just a pattern we are experiencing. The names and faces change, but it is still the same pattern, and it must be surrendered if we are to grow and experience our Divinity.

Surrender is the exchange we give back to the Divine for that which it is trying to give us. Surrender is never easy, because we do not get to choose what we will have to give up. By the Grace of the Divine, some depth of contraction (that we were not even aware of) has now emerged so that we can do the work to be free of it. Those deeper and deeper patterns are the real issue. God does not want your money, your body, or your mind. God wants your heart, simply to fill it up. It is not the mind that surrenders; it is the mind that is surrendered. We cannot surrender in our mind because it is limited, and represents the ego. The mind cannot feel God—only the heart can reach that depth. And it is only when we can feel our heart that we can surrender.

Every day, we have situations in which we make choices. We have the choice to hold on to that which limits and contracts us, or we can let go of those boundaries. We must have the simple intelligence and the honesty to say, "This thing is really keeping me wrapped too tight." Be honest with yourself and reach to receive the Grace that is trying to manifest for you in your life. Then the whole picture changes and surrender is not the negative thing we imagine it to be—it is a joyous opportunity to let go, again and again.

USING THE ENERGY TO RISE ABOVE OUR LIMITATIONS

When we surrender something we do not just throw it into the garbage heap. We have to consciously extract energy out of the dynamic and use that energy as inner fuel. We simply let go of it—and then draw its energy back into our psychic mechanism and put it into the flow. And although it hurts and is challenging and makes us crazy, every time we want to grab it again we use our discipline to re-center ourselves and pull the energy back inside. We are surrendering our limitations and our inability to see from a higher perspective, so we must do this work on a purely energetic level, without attaching any mental or emotional content to it. In effect, we are surrendering our reality, which includes all our ingrained patterns.

If we hold on to our limitations we cannot extract anything from them. A pattern is trapped energy. Letting go of the pattern is simply releasing the energy, and we can then pull it into our heart and absorb it. We work like the python that has to digest a large animal, using our inner chemistry to break down an enormous meal, converting it into nourishment. We are feeding growth in ourselves and bringing that experience into a deeper place inside. From there, we can see everything from a different perspective, although for a while, the energy may still feel like a big, half-assimilated lump. It takes some time to digest it, and while this is happening we have to continually surrender in order to transcend the pattern and complete the change.

Not only must we let go, but once we've done that, we have to be vigilant not to grab on again. The problem is that our limitations have become our comfort zone. Those limitations define who we think we are, and we are very attached to that definition. Sometimes what we surrender seems to stick to us like fly paper, and we can't shake it loose. It requires discipline to keep on shaking and not reengage, but if we continue to let go, we will transmute the energy of the pattern.

Our tensions will never give up if we keep reinforcing them. We are not letting go if we continually revisit some tension by trying to understand and analyze it, or if we need to blame somebody for what has happened. These are all indications that we have not surrendered deeply enough. This concept goes against some of today's conventional wisdom, but we do not need to engage our tensions to be free of them. We don't need to do anything except surrender and pull the energy back inside. By doing this, we take full responsibility for the state we are in. We surrender anything that keeps us separate from our own Divine Source.

A TANTRIC UNDERSTANDING OF STILLNESS

The entire consideration of surrender can best be framed in these terms: *Stillness is the doorway into the vibrating presence that is the Divine, and surrender is the key to the door.* I have discussed the idea that we surrender in order to reveal the highest reality within us, to move beyond the limited egoic belief in the duality of the inner and outer world. Our individuated consciousness, being no less and no different than Divine Consciousness, is the means to uncovering this highest reality within—and through discriminating awareness, we can experience and express Divine Consciousness as the world.

The Tantric Spandakarikas discuss what is called *spanda*, which describes how all of life arises from the infinitesimally subtle pulsation that is simply the vibrancy of consciousness. All of life emerges from this center stillpoint, and at first there is only the intent to express. Then, from that intent, manifestation appears.

Arising out of the power within Pure Consciousness—in the pulsation created from awareness—life emerges. We are That, but of course, from the perspective of Unity, we are the Source as well. The discussion of *spanda,* or vibrating Presence, helps us understand and ultimately experience that our life is completely an expression of this dynamic of consciousness.

Stillness and surrender are not separate from each other. They arise and subside within Presence. We first tune in to a stillpoint in the center of our heart, but because everything is happening on the field of consciousness, on a field of vibrating Presence, we can learn to find that stillpoint everywhere. If we lose contact with our center we can, through surrender, tune back inside at any time and find stillness. Then, as we extend our inner state out into the dynamics we encounter, we experience that life arises and subsides in, on, and as this field of consciousness.

THE PAIN OF FORGETTING, THE JOY OF REMEMBERING

If all of life is an expression of Consciousness, how can the ego be separate from its own Source, the Divine Reality? In truth it can't be—yet isn't it amazing that not only is our experience one of separation, but the ego also claims agency to that separation and becomes a warrior, defending its kingdom. Our spiritual work is to be able to witness, explore, and recognize what an incredible dichotomy exists between God's experience of what He created, and our limited experience of the same creation.

Through Śiva's Divine Will to create and enjoy the universe, He hid Himself and proclaimed, "I can't recognize myself anymore." And He did this just for the fun of it, for what Shaivism calls "the play of Consciousness." From our perspective, we can't help but wonder, "Couldn't He have created the Divine Play, without forgetting?" The fact that He purposely forgot suggests that so much of the fun and joy is in the remembering. The gift God gave each of us is that through us He remembers who He is.

We have the power within ourselves to create our own life, moment by moment. The critical question is whether this is a conscious creation or an unconscious one. If we wish to make a truly conscious choice, we must abide in stillness and surrender. It is only when we are established in this state that we are able to experience Divine Will—the explosion of Consciousness into creation that occurs simply because the Divine chose to manifest.

The problem we encounter is that as we engage in life, we get lost in the field of manifestation. We move farther from our center and forget our Source. When we do remember, we can always refocus our awareness within. We use our capacity to know ourselves, to get in touch with a deeper aspect of the experience we are having. Another way of saying this is that we turn inside—although again, this expression exposes a limitation of language because there is no inside or outside. There is only the functioning of our consciousness in its own field, which is an exponentially expanding state of openness.

When openness is not our experience, we must recognize that it is through our own will that we are closed. The Divine Will, which manifests everything in creation, has given us the same will to decide how we experience that creation. It is only we who choose to close. We can blame God for having given us free will and limited consciousness, or we can surrender our individual will and expand our consciousness. In a liberated state we can then resolve all apparent paradoxes regarding the nature of will—from God's perspective. Wouldn't it be an amazing thing to experience that all of life is made up of consciousness, never diminished from its Source, or its own infinity?

CREATING THE HIGHEST LIFE FOR OURSELVES

Consciousness has two inseparable qualities. Consciousness is both the Source and the power of life, and also contains the capacity for Self-awareness. This second aspect has direct implications for our own lives, because it brings home the message that if we have the will to do anything we want, we need to be aware of what we are creating. Unfortunately, it is often only after we have lost our center that we realize we weren't paying attention, and have generated a different experience than the one we intended. The fact that we might do this from an unconscious versus a conscious state only demonstrates that we have free will to choose between those two options. And it further illustrates that becoming conscious is the means to transforming life. Even a glimpse of this understanding creates an immediate shift in us. We begin to remember what is most important in life, and as we do so, we surrender, and let go.

Living in contact with an internal place of surrender and stillness gives us the power to rise above our limited point of view. When we find ourselves not understanding, or blaming somebody else for something we think they did to us, we have the capacity to stop and say, "I remember something . . . I created my own life." Life never happens to you. It only happens from within you. Always.

When we really absorb this fact, we begin to let go of our perspective. We stop defending, and stop holding on to what binds us. Without that understanding, we behave like the women in the 1950s ads for Lucky Strike cigarettes, who would "rather fight than switch." We would rather fight, defend, judge, attack, and react, based on our personal limitations—and all of those defenses are one gigantic effort to prove that what we think, know, and feel is valid, correct, and the center of the universe.

We must find stillness in our desire, even in the state of contraction, so that we do not act from a place of constriction. The impulse of *spanda* creates everything we experience. *Spanda* arises as our need, desire, pain, and every individual reaction we firmly hold on to, but it also gives us openness and clarity. Because every experience is arising and subsiding on our own field of consciousness, it is critical to recognize that we do not have to do anything with the manifestation. When we can rest in the stillpoint and stay centered in a state of openness, we develop the ability to move through our limited perspective. Then, when a new thought begins to arise, as the contraction begins to take place, as the fear begins to consume us, we can stay in that stillpoint and watch everything unfold. The entire dynamic can take place in our center because we are in a state of stillness, and whatever unfolds does not necessitate a reaction.

LIVING FROM THE INTERNAL STILLPOINT

When we are established in the stillpoint, we do not lose ourselves as our awareness is extended outward. The energy may extend, but it simply arises and subsides back into the stillpoint without us attaching ourselves to the manifestation. We avoid creating some dynamic that pulls us out of our center, thereby requiring us to refocus and come back in. This is another way to describe surrender. It means that surrender happens because we have the capacity to use our consciousness to reach into stillness and not leave that state, even as all the dynamics of life appear before us.

We must, however, also learn to consciously extend ourselves into life for the purpose of more expansion. We can't try to reject the world in the attempt to find stillness. Instead, we simply carry the stillpoint outward, never forgetting our own essence as we move through the dynamics of life.

A person who lives in a state of stillness is someone who can move through any situation and never forget that they are God. Until we are able to function on that level, understand that no matter how far we have strayed from our center, no matter how big the contraction or pattern, or how often it has been repeated, there is never a moment that stillness doesn't exist right there and then. We can always return to center from any distance, because in reality, there is no distance between the field of consciousness and any manifestation of creation.

Stillness is found between the rising and subsiding of each pulsation. There is no difference between what is found at the beginning and at the end of each pulsation. Using our discriminating awareness, we can feel the stillpoint around which all experience happens. When we tune in to and align ourselves with that place and keep our attention there, we can experience the rising and subsiding without ever leaving our center.

The stillpoint and pulsation ultimately feel like a state of openness, and in this expansiveness the pulsation is so subtle that it is almost not there. Throughout our practice we tune in to this by focusing our consciousness and allowing our awareness to be absorbed back into its own Self. Sometimes we will predominantly feel the stillpoint and other times we'll be more aware of the pulsation. In either case we keep letting go, simply focusing our consciousness into an even more subtle stillpoint. Then, as we feel the state of stillness and Presence, we can use the flow to lift the energy up. When we feed the energy of flow into consciousness, our awareness expands. This is the process that repeats itself over and over again, allowing us to grow.

THE ARISING AND SUBSIDING OF ENERGY

Life offers us endless feedback at every moment, but we are so attached to our point of view that we don't even remember to listen to it. When we become still, we can tune our internal radio dial past the static, pick up a clear signal, and hear the message. We can receive the signal when we stop talking, stop reacting, and stop fighting. Surrender only happens when we are not busy defending our limited perspective. We cannot do both at the same time. Have the courage to stop fighting to protect your position. I have a standing joke with my students that the technique for not reacting is to wrap duct tape over their mouths. This means having the discipline—every time we feel a tension or contraction starting to arise—to back off and simply not act. Then the tension subsides back into the stillpoint.

In the discussion of *spanda*, the pulsation was described as that which emerges, expands, and falls back, all within the field of consciousness. Similarly, our actions and reactions, mind and emotions, are just energy that arises and either gives form to something—or, if we don't attach to the energy, subsides back into itself. In other words, the need to react is not inherent in the arising and subsiding; it is a form that can develop only if we attach content to the energy. If we don't attach content, then there is nothing to create tension or misunderstanding. There is simply an energy field rising and subsiding back into the stillpoint.

Using subtle discrimination, we can become aware of the impulse as it arises, in the very moment of its inception. The pulsation is the natural expression of what is creating our individuated life. It has no content, yet we habitually apply content to it. By resting in stillness, we gain the capacity to be aware of that pulsation as pure energy, and to let go before it ever crystallizes into content. This requires a lot of stillness, a lot of practice, and the focusing of our consciousness. As soon as an impulse starts to arise, before it gets out of control and creates an action we might regret, we let go and surrender it.

Because the same stillness exists everywhere, the point of surrender is also available everywhere, in the midst of any activity. No matter what activity we are involved in, it is our minds that take us out of stillness. We believe our thoughts, and we then defend our position instead of letting go. Only Consciousness and energy exist. Our thoughts are only forms that emerge from energy. When we recognize that energy doesn't have to solidify into any manifest form, we can watch it arise and subside without attaching thought to it. The Sanskrit term for this capacity is *nirvikalpa samādhi*, the thought-free state.

We have to pay attention to form and content in order to function in the world, but we should not get caught up in thinking that this is the only reality. If we do lose ourselves in some dynamic, our center is always accessible at any point. Consciousness is there inside us, always and forever. No matter how tense we get or how contracted and bound in a pattern we are, with self-awareness we can immediately redirect our attention.

When we become really experienced, we can, with one breath, bring ourselves back into our center. Even though the situation we are facing may not change, we change our relationship to it by changing our focus. It is always our own consciousness that either binds us or frees us. When we are quiet we become fully aware of which choice we are feeding.

THE MAHA-MANTRA

The discussion of surrender always boils down to one question: What do we want most out of this life? People are so concerned about what they will have to give up, or won't have, or won't be able to do, etc., etc. My response is always that it is not a question of what we have to give up if we surrender; it is what we give up if we don't. I have previously referred to what Swami Chetanananda termed the mantra of stupidity, "What's gonna happen to me?" Here's what I call the Maha-Mantra: "I know that if I surrender, I will find complete freedom—but I'm still not going to do it . . . and no one can make me."

If freedom, unconditional joy, and fulfillment are what we want, then whatever we have to surrender seems petty in comparison. Surrender is simply letting go of all that binds us, and exactly *what* binds us is irrelevant. If we come up against it and we are not willing to let go, then we are accepting the limitation. So we surrender in order to get closer to our center, to merge into the infinite field of consciousness.

For this to happen, our own individual consciousness must be cracked open, expanded, and transformed. We must surrender everything that does not allow us to change—everything that binds and limits our consciousness, including our attachment to that perspective. We have to surrender the part of us that thinks it knows reality, and then holds on to and defends that position at all cost.

Surrender is not negative. The deepest part of us already knows and recognizes that we are not the designer of our life. When we stubbornly hold on to our limited perspective, when we reject what arises in the dynamics of living, what happens? We generally end up with a lot of knots in the fabric of the life we are weaving. In order to change we have to be willing to accept, admit, and look for the possibility that the experience we are having may not be the fullest possible. If we are not actually experiencing that we are the infinite field of consciousness, there is something limiting our own experience.

REACHING FOR A DEEPER LEVEL OF SURRENDER

Surrender is a mature expression of our consciousness, but we must bring surrender into the equation from the very first day we start our practice. If we don't begin now, when will we develop that capacity? Rudi gave us many gifts and one of the greatest was his death. I can tell you it took a lot of surrender to deal with that event. I was only twenty-two years old when Rudi's plane smashed into the side of a mountain. If I had not been able to find surrender at that moment, my practice would almost certainly have been derailed. We can't let ourselves get caught in the idea "I'll do better next time." The ability to surrender will mature over time, but the powerful technique of surrendering into stillness is available right now, at any stage of one's practice.

Whatever the level of surrender we are dealing with, when we hear ourselves think, "I can't surrender this," it means we are buying into our limited perspective. If Rudi had come to me the day before he got in the plane and said, "Tomorrow I am checking out," I probably could not have dealt with it. I could not have gotten past my mind, my fear, my attachment to him, everything. I would have locked him in a closet.

What is the difference between knowing the day before, and the moment at two in the morning when I heard that he had left his body? I didn't have time to project. How I was able, within five minutes of hearing that, to let go and feel incredible joy, I cannot tell you. It was only Grace. I wasn't that smart and I didn't have forty years of practice in surrender.

What an incredible gift it was to be able to see past my limited perspective and the pain of losing my teacher, and recognize that

Rudi was free! It was a gift, and yet surrendering Rudi's physical presence was gut-wrenching and not something I had been prepared to do.

THE GREATEST OBSTACLE WE FACE IS OURSELVES

There is a section of a Kabir poem that says,

> We sense that there is some sort of spirit
> that loves birds and animals and the ants —
> perhaps the same one who gave radiance
> to you in your mother's womb.
> Is it logical you would be walking around
> entirely orphaned now?
> The truth is you turned away yourself,
> and decided to go into the dark alone.

We must not let ourselves become our own limitation. We can't let our minds convince us that we have to do one thing or another before we can be free. It is not true. If we can create the discipline to not act on our perspective, we will begin to experience a much higher perspective. When we feel ourselves starting to act from a narrow viewpoint, we must remember that we do not have to go down that road. As we surrender through nonaction, some deeper innate consciousness begins to inform us. The God within us begins to be revealed.

Those who have been engaged in spiritual practice for many years need to be aware of the tendency to defend the fact they have not yet achieved their liberation. We want to validate the idea that there is a lengthy process we have to go through. Of course, there *is* a process we have to undertake, but I am simply suggesting that perhaps unconditional surrender is that process. When considering our spiritual freedom we must get beyond the limiting notion that it must take a long time.

I've mentioned Abhinavagupta's amazing statement that in four sessions of forty minutes we can achieve realization. He was not a person who would say something like this lightly. He said that with a deep enough wish, with the profound focusing of our consciousness, we can tune in to the highest reality and be free at any time. The only thing standing in our way is our attachment to our limitations. This is what we must surrender.

The question is: If we are free already, how can it be true that we have to burn through all our encumbrances in order to experience our freedom? It is a conundrum. I once heard the story of a saint who had attained his freedom after doing *sādhana* for forty years. When asked whether one had to practice specific techniques in order to gain liberation, he said, "No . . . but I wouldn't have known this if I hadn't practiced for all those years."

A DEEPER UNDERSTANDING OF TENSION

Within the discussion of stillness and surrender, we can revisit and add to the previous consideration of transcending our tensions and patterns. Remember that tensions are primarily created by energy that is not in flow. It is our resistance, our inability to accept life as it is, that produces tension. Whenever there is a reaction to circumstance and condition—whenever we are unable to truly rest in the stillness of our center and accept something as it is—we get tense because we want to control what is happening.

Every situation in our life emerges from our heart as a part of the process of freeing us. These dynamics free us from the limited perspective that continually insists, "I don't accept life as it is." Rudi's response to this was beautifully expressed when he said, "Those who pick apart the thread weaken the fabric of creation by applying their mind to the design, because to them God's will is not acceptable as their own." Stubbornly holding on to our perspective, and getting tense whenever something happens that does not meet our expectations, is the opposite of surrender.

As was the case with the imprisoned Tibetan monk, whose only concern was to keep his heart open, we must choose how we react to what life presents us, even if situations appear to be difficult. Every day we let ourselves get caught up in conditions and then get tense because the conditions aren't what we think they ought to be. It's a pattern of behavior that is self-perpetuating. We keep doing it because it's the only way we've known to deal with life. The fact that it may be hard to let go of our tensions is again not relevant. The part of us that wants freedom has to become stronger than the part that does not. It is our reaction to what happens that either limits or doesn't limit us.

So when we find ourselves getting tense, that's the time to surrender. We begin by letting go of at least some of the tension, from a deep enough inner place, to even remember to take a breath. Two things are then happening. First, we are using our consciousness to say, "It just isn't worth it. I have to let go." Then, we have to start creating some breath and some space from which to let go on a deeper level. By doing the double-breath with an awareness of what we need to surrender, we can allow the energy to be transmuted into something that feeds our growth.

Freedom comes from surrendering. It will not come otherwise. We must be willing to surrender for more than three seconds. Then, we must surrender the second time and the third time . . . and the thousandth time that something binds us—particularly when it is the same thing that binds us over and over again. It will keep binding us until we completely rise above it.

WE MUST SURRENDER OUR PATTERNS

I have described patterns as the things we do repeatedly that keep us separate from God. Just as tensions have varying levels of intensity, our patterns have different depths. We must deal with the patterns we recognize, but because patterns reflect the incredible capacity of the ego to veil our truest nature, it really is this deeper issue we need to address. And although patterns often show up as repeated behavior, our actions are not really the issue. What is of more concern is the pattern from which the behavior arises, as well as the source of the pattern itself.

The content we experience is not in the pattern, but is merely its effect. We can let go of our limited perspective, immediately, from wherever we are stuck. In the same way, we can surrender our patterns if we choose to do so. We do not have to go through the gross expression of an experience in order to learn. The question is only how far from center we allow ourselves to get before tuning back inside. By believing that we must follow through with some reaction, we justify continually doing so.

Our deep internal patterns include judgment, doubt, and fear, and these are what we need to release. What is the essence of fear? It is apprehension about the unknown, about changing our experience—because if we change that experience, it won't continue to reinforce our understanding of life. How subtle is that? This is how the ego works. It is always trying to make everything fit its limited perspective. The tension that arises from attachment to our perspective is just energy, but if we don't burn it up, it becomes a force that grinds a deeper pattern and groove within us. We have interior crevices the depth of the Grand Canyon because we keep reinforcing them, giving them life and energy through holding on to our tensions. In this way we continually reinforce our patterns, and as they cut deeper and deeper we become completely unconscious of them.

Whenever we are caught in something superficial and get tense in our attempt to control life, we forget. We don't recognize that the tension is really the bubbling up of the deeper constriction of our patterns. We have to understand that these patterns come from lifetime after lifetime. The very deepest tension is the separation from God and the anger resulting from that isolation. Self-rejection is the highest form of reinforcing our separation, and it usually shows up as self-destruction. But we always have the power to choose how we deal with the dynamics we face. Every time a pattern shows up, instead of reinforcing it and thereby destroying the opportunity to change, we can work to free ourselves of it.

SEEING OUR PATTERNS BEFORE THEY FULLY ARISE

The first thing we do to change a pattern is recognize it. Again, not necessarily the content or the details, but the fact that there is an underlying pattern happening. We may observe that we keep finding ourselves in the same place. If we stop and get quiet as soon as we see the repetition arising, we can sense the energy of it. Like every bar on the face of the earth, it has the same resonance. When we recognize the feeling—which usually involves a sense of compressing, contracting, and closing our heart—we can start to free the energy and open to it. If we get caught in the detail and the content, we can't unbind the energy, and we miss the chance to free the pattern.

If we don't get still and surrender, our patterns become like tidal waves that hit us by surprise. So we must develop the capacity to feel a pattern as it starts to surface. If we then surrender into the internal stillpoint, we can dissolve the pattern the moment it starts to re-create itself. Once a tidal wave hits us by surprise, we can only hold on for dear life, and pray that we land somewhere in one piece with enough consciousness to spot the wave the next time it swells. It is only when we can recognize and let go of a pattern as it first arises that we avoid giving it more energy to repeat itself. Once we are able to be still and centered inside we can feel a pattern coming from a long way away. It is like seeing an approaching storm from a distance and getting out of its path.

The more energy a pattern has—the deeper it is ingrained in us—the greater the consciousness we have to bring to its release. If we can't completely release something, at least we can move it up a notch by creating a new pattern with the energy as it starts to emerge. As you start to go crazy and want to react, just stop and say, "No, I am not going to do this." Do something consciously to divert the energy, so it does not manifest in the same way. In effect, this replaces one pattern with a lesser one, but it's still a means of freeing ourselves from energy that is stuck in a particular dimension.

WE CAN RELEASE EVEN THE DEEPEST PATTERNS

If we deeply let go, we can release any pattern, even if it has been in us for a long time. Beginning when I was five years old, I was terribly afraid of going to sleep because I had a recurring nightmare three to four nights a week. I would experience watching what I can only describe as a field of nothingness—and all of a sudden, a single speck of dust would come floating down through the air. It would come down and stop, then separate and start going farther and farther away, getting bigger and bigger and bigger, uglier and uglier, more and more powerful, becoming two humongous balls of energy and sound, moving away from me . . . . The next thing I knew they were coming at me, about to smash me. And every night, just as the energy balls were about to hit, I woke up screaming bloody murder. It was a really, really frightening experience.

At about age fourteen, the nightmares stopped. But the first time I sat down in class with Rudi, guess what happened? All of a sudden that field manifested in front of me again and there was that speck of dust . . . and the whole nightmare began again. I somehow had the presence of mind to let go as the two massive balls were about to obliterate me. I just let go. And they simply dissolved. I felt an incredible stillness and peace. I immediately understood that the fear and pain of the one speck separating and becoming two and moving into infinity, gathering more and more strength, was my inner experience of being separated from

God. I understood that the fear of being smashed was my ego's terror of being dissolved, its fear of allowing me to move back into Unity.

It was amazing to me, because this happened during my very first class with Rudi. It certainly made me recognize that something unusual was going on in meeting my teacher, and it was a profound lesson in the power of consciousness to transform one's experience, even in the face of deep fear and patterns. This was a very early realization in my spiritual journey, demonstrating that the soul's pain of separation and the longing to be reunited is equally matched by the egoic fear of being dissolved. This is why it is so important that we remain aware of our power to choose, because we must consciously choose Oneness instead of fear. This fear may manifest as a pattern of behavior, but we must always look for the deeper source of our experiences.

ALIGNING OURSELVES WITH GOD'S WILL

We cannot discuss stillness and surrender without revisiting the topic of service. True surrender expresses our willingness to serve the highest part of ourselves, instead of continually serving something less. Rudi learned this lesson at a very early age. At about eight years old, he started having visitations from Tibetan lamas while he was sleeping. This continued for a number of years, with the lamas repeatedly placing vessels containing secret teachings (known as *Tormas*) in Rudi's body. At one point they essentially told him, "We have finished installing these *Tormas*, but if you want this hidden knowledge to surface, you must serve God. You must teach until the day you die and you should never ever forget, like most people do, that you are not serving the world—you are serving God." What an incredible experience to have as a child!

In order to know when an action will truly serve God, we again must become very still. When we extend ourselves and look past our own needs, we let go of our tensions about controlling life. We surrender the patterns we might otherwise keep repeating. In fact, we have to let go of them in order to have enough energy to extend ourselves. The content of this resistance is never relevant. We must have the capacity to center ourselves and not repeat "What's gonna happen to me?" in the context of whatever is being asked of us. When we surrender our tensions and patterns we can serve from a place of love, gratitude, and devotion.

In essence, doing service is practice for surrendering our individual will. Everyone knows the distinct resonance of imposing their own will versus surrendering and letting a higher intelligence show itself and provide guidance. The key to understanding the surrendering of our will is that it involves redirecting our life force. When an impulse to act arises, we let go of it while remaining in the stillness of our center. If it surfaces again, we surrender it again and again. At a certain point, it will be crystal clear if a particular impulse reflects a manifestation of the highest part of us, or if it arises from some limitation. But until we have that clarity, we continue to let go.

Surrendering our own will comes from the depth of our consciousness, completely beyond the level of "Should I do this, or should I do that?" Established in stillness, we trust God enough to hand over our perspective. In time, we shift away from any fear about losing our will, because we see that what we are actually doing is surrendering to the highest will. From this new vantage point, it becomes evident that what we are really surrendering is our separate identity. Getting past the resistance to letting go of our separateness will undoubtedly break a few bones. Nevertheless, we have to surrender.

Surrender is like diving off a high board. We may not know how to execute a graceful double flip, and we may be afraid to take the plunge—but we can at least jump. The alternatives are to stand there frozen with fear or retreat back down the steps. Once we get over our fear and finally jump, we generally get out of the water and immediately climb back up again. But sometimes when we jump, it's as if God has suddenly sucked the water out of the pool, and we go splat.

God is smarter than we are and this impact may be necessary to jar loose the grip our ego has on us. Our only response should be to stop fighting and stop thinking we are the doer. God is in charge, and He is doing a perfect job of providing us with whatever we need to attain our freedom. If we complain, worry, or fear the process, we are rejecting the Grace that has manifested as the difficult experiences we face. God shoves those obstacles at us because they are exactly what we need to expose and dissolve the intensity of contraction, density, and karma we have created for ourselves through lifetimes of holding on.

The ego never changes, and the ego itself never gets enlightened. There is only the dissolution of its fundamental misunderstanding. We let go of every arising tension, every pattern and contraction that we experience in life—because we understand that all of this is the effect of the ego's intent to protect its status. All the acts in the epic dramas of our lives are just scenes in the ever-popular play entitled *I Am Separate*.

The quickest way to intimately know God is to surrender our separateness, and we do this is by letting go of everything else. We surrender everything that keeps us separate from God until the egoic vise that has been gripping us has nothing to hold on to.

THE FORCES OF CONCEALMENT AND REVELATION

Tantric philosophy describes the Fivefold Acts of the Divine, which are continuously happening: creation, maintenance, dissolution, concealment, and revelation. God's presence is a vibration that is perpetually arising and subsiding. Inherent in that vibration is a consciousness that can conceal or reveal the underlying reality of life. We live through that same process—expanding, contracting, and repeating a pattern. The Divine is always present, always within us as ourselves, so we are performing the same acts as God, every day and every moment of our lives.

All of our experiences can be understood in terms of this pulsation. Something arises, we experience it, and then it subsides again. Creation, maintenance, and dissolution are present all the time, and the nature of our experience is determined by whether we are focused on the act of concealment or the act of revelation. Without our awareness of it, the pulsation would be like the proverbial tree falling in the forest. If God hadn't created conscious life, there would be no one to appreciate this amazing act of manifestation.

We become aware of this pulsation as we tune in to the essential vibrancy of life, which is the deepest level of who we are. The pulsation is always happening on the field of our consciousness, but we may not be aware of it. This is because there is also another force, another set of energies at work, which is either concealing our true nature—making us feel we are separate and different from the pulsation—or revealing that Unity to us. This is why I've said that the consciousness within a human being has the same power to obscure reality as it does to reveal it. It's another way of stating that concealment and revelation are different powers of the same consciousness. When we focus on revelation we consciously allow Grace to guide our lives.

From God's point of view, He was simply pulsating as unbounded Consciousness, thinking, "Okay, there has got to be more fun than this." So what did he do? He created the entire manifest universe as an act of concealment. He surrendered His awareness of Himself. The universe is an act of concealment, even though it surfaces from and is not different from its Source. Looking at the effulgent creation, we get caught in the intricacies of the world and get stuck there, thinking it is different from us.

The world isn't inherently bad. It is Divine celebration, and yet manifestation has within it the capacity to conceal its own true Self. Seen in terms of revelation, the universe is not different than Itself; it is simply the pulsation of our consciousness. But just as God, through His free will, concealed Himself in order to have the joy of remembering, we do the same.

We can either get lost in blaming ourselves for forgetting—which invokes a whole litany of self-rejection, guilt, and the immersion in our tensions—or we can recognize that there is no need for censure. Concealment and revelation are simply flip sides of the process of gaining our freedom. Spiritual growth is learning that we are the very same consciousness that concealed our own Unity. Then, the joy is in the remembering.

I have said that one of the aspects of consciousness is the capacity for self-awareness. We become conscious of whether we are concealing or whether we are revealing. Our acts of concealment manifest as our limited perceptions, tensions, and patterns, and as our unwillingness to serve and to surrender our own separateness. Yet those very acts of concealment are the means to the revelation. We either choose to live in the concealment of what that process is bringing to us, or in the Grace and revelation of the growth being made available.

SURRENDER TO THE MYSTERY OF GOD

We need to understand the subtle difference in our own experience between concealment and revelation. What shifts us is stillness and surrender. Revelation is described as Grace, which is the freedom-bestowing power of the Divine. So while pulsation and concealment are in progress, we might imagine God sitting somewhere doing His calculations, musing, "When will I reveal to this person his own true nature?" Wouldn't it be amazing to realize that the freedom-bestowing power of the Divine is not separate from you? *Śaktipāta* is described as the descent of Grace, but where does it actually descend from? You. This paradox reflects the mystery of consciousness.

None of us can answer the fundamental question of who created the Divine. How can It always have been there? It's a mystery. If such a vast intelligence could always have existed and from that, the entire universe was created, then there ought to be room for a few mysteries in our lives. If revelation is the act of Divine Grace, we must simply get out of the way and let it happen, by trusting and surrendering to that highest consciousness.

All of the fivefold acts are unfolding simultaneously. While the act of concealment casts its veil over our consciousness, revelation at the same time uncovers it. How we experience this interplay really boils down to our choice of where we focus our consciousness—on concealment or on revelation. In the face of such a magnificent display of the Divine, we can only surrender and open our hearts. Devotion is an ecstatic expression of pure joy and gratitude. From a place of stillness, we can only wish to offer ourselves.

Nityananda said that the difference between the individual and the universal is like that of a river and the ocean into which it flows. The water is the same. There is only an apparent difference. Dissolution of even that subtle distinction takes place through surrender, when the individual self merges and dissolves into the universal. There are endless reasons not to surrender and only one reason to do so—because we wish to be free.

Surrender is the joyous offering of ourselves to God and the letting go of any obstacle that gets in the way of fulfilling that highest aspiration. I have been talking about surrendering our limited perspective and surrendering our will—and we all have the freedom to choose how to respond to that opportunity. Our answer can be anything from, "I just won't do it" to "I surrender myself completely." The choice is ours to make. We can only enter into this depth of surrender on the field of our own consciousness. If we truly take a vow to find that state of awareness, then we meet whatever comes along in the moment and say, "I let go of this, I let go of that." It is possible to do this, and yet most people do not.

If surrender is the highest act of freedom and choice, the highest act of consciousness, then God's act of surrender, of forgetting Himself, was the supreme act. He did it for the profound joy of remembering. What is your life about—the joy of remembering, or the pain of having forgotten? We get to choose whether we live in joy or pain. When we choose living in God's heart, there is both the outer expression of surrender and the inner experience of Oneness. And without that inner experience, we cannot truly surrender.

The key to the doorway of surrender is an open heart, and beyond this door is our treasure. Sometimes we misplace the key, only to discover that it has been hanging around our neck all the time. What could be a higher aspiration in life than transforming our consciousness and experiencing Divine Presence? The essence of spiritual practice is surrendering to that Divine Force. When you learn to surrender and live in stillness, you will recognize life as a magnificent celebration of God's Grace.

LIVING IN THE
HEART OF STILLNESS

10

CHAPTER TEN

Learning to live in the stillness of the heart is central to spiritual growth, and looking at our journey from this perspective helps tie together many of the ideas already presented in this book. *Kuṇḍalinī sādhana* provides us with the tools to contact this deepest resonance of our heart—both during our meditation and as we extend ourselves out into the world. We anchor ourselves in our center, in the stillness of our heart, and this is what creates a profound, permanent immersion into the heart of God.

We see this level of attainment in the lives of all saints, and it is delineated and explored in all great traditions. At the core of Tantric teaching is the knowledge that liberation occurs within every individual when their own individual consciousness is merged into the Divine. Bhagavan Nityananda provides the inspiration for this state of realization in my lineage of teachers.

Living as a pure manifestation of the Divine, Nityananda described what he called the "heart-space," or the "sky of the heart"—the consciousness created when *Kuṇḍalinī* has risen to create a single, united openness in the *cakras* in the heart, center of the head, and crown. Nityananda said, "The heart is the most sacred of all places, go there and roam." The purity, simplicity, and joy that radiated from him because of this experience unleashed an extraordinary Presence and Grace, which affected tens of thousands of people in his lifetime.

Stillness is the doorway into God's heart, and we find this entryway through our own consciousness when we experience:

- the stillness of breath
- the stillness of awareness
- the stillness of desire
- the stillness of will

Divine Presence is within each of us, always available in every moment to anyone who wishes to connect to it. It is not just the purview of extraordinary saints such as Nityananda. They are simply a beacon, shining a light on what is accessible to everyone. We all have the Divine right to live in that state. The immersion into the heart-space is at once a technical process—the development of the capacity to focus our awareness into the deepest stillpoint within us—and also the expression of understanding that comes from making contact with stillness. Presence is revealed from within each of us if we can bring stillness to every dimension of our lives.

THE STILLNESS OF BREATH

As we become very still inside we are able to feel the vibrating radiance of consciousness from which all levels of breath arise and unfold. We experience the internal breath, which is the very power of life, arising and subsiding within us. This breath of life creates our body and our physical breath from within itself. What appears to be the body and gross breath is really an effect of this pulsation of vitality, which is ever-flowing in the *suṣumṇa*. In stillness, we can notice each internal breath lifting our vital force from the base of the spine, up through the *suṣumṇa*, and into the center of the head, without ever taking a physical breath.

When we tune in to the internal breath we are not breathing in and out. The breath is entirely within the *suṣumṇa*, and this is why the experience is ultimately not one of breathing, but of being breathed. There is an incredible line in one of the Nityananda sutras that says,

> *Those who do not breathe through the nostrils have no desire. When, with practice, the breath is controlled, it becomes centered in the suṣumṇa. The breath is purely internal and joy and bliss flow within. When the sādhaka draws up the internal breath to the heart-space he realizes himself as the Self.*

Established in stillness of breath, our awareness is still, our desires are still, and our will is still. Desire is for something other, outside of us. Even the desire for an external breath is a reflection of our limited perception that breathing in and out is what gives us life. When we recognize that we are being breathed by God we are fulfilled and have no sense of lack, and therefore no desires. We realize we are alive because of the Grace of God.

The internal breath within us gives rise to the gross breath, which gives life to the body. But when the gross breath stops and the body dies, we do not die. Only the particular body we have been using falls away. Consciousness remains, because Life Itself never ceases to exist.

Experiencing stillness of breath takes practice. Even the internal breath is the effect of consciousness. It arises from a stillpoint, begins to vibrate, and becomes the form of our gross breath. Discriminating awareness is necessary to find the stillpoint of consciousness—and then we must surrender into that Presence in order to feel the internal breath arising. This is what creates a permanent internal awareness, which is the basis of changing our experience of life.

THE STILLNESS OF AWARENESS

Stillness of awareness is a critical capacity that any authentic spiritual aspirant must develop. We learn to rest in our center, watch, and say, "I see and understand what is happening. I don't have to engage this dynamic in order to free myself from it." In fact, this is the fastest way out of any misunderstanding, because when we are not caught in the drama, we avoid being overwhelmed over and over again by the same energy. When the whirlwind we face is almost more intense than we can bear, it is a reflection of how tightly we are holding on to not being free.

We must make the choice to move beyond our patterns and tensions. We cannot allow them to dictate our experience. If we either get caught in emotional turmoil or try to numb our pain (through whatever means), we are denying ourselves the opportunity to be free. Rudi always said, "Pain is God loving you." He meant that all the experiences in our lives are Divinely offered as the means to freedom—not just the blissful ones. The most intense difficulties contain the biggest opportunity for liberation. When we are able to abide in stillness, we can simply witness the merry-go-round of our tensions, patterns, and struggles, and recognize that they are our attempt to remain bound.

Find that stillness of awareness. This is the platform from which we can make truly conscious choices. My advice is that when you are not in a place of stillness, don't make any choices, and don't spew negativity and tension onto the people who love you. When we are reactive, we either end up apologizing later, or we justify ourselves by saying, "You deserve it . . . it's your fault!" Open and surrender until you find stillness inside. Otherwise the effect of our action is the creation of karma. This is not something we can postpone doing until some future time, thinking, "I am not yet strong enough." It is always now, in this moment, that we must be willing to let go and be changed. We are either growing or not growing. When we doubt and second-guess, it is just a sign that the ego is trying to grip us.

Profound transformation happens because we change inside. We can change our behavior—and that can give us some clue as to what our life should look like. But we have to be careful when doing this because we are projecting what our behavior and experience *should* be, based only on our imagination about something we have yet to experience. We are projecting based on our limited awareness. Still, we do need the discipline to work and make conscious choices even when we have not yet found a higher level of inner consciousness. We develop a willingness to function from a deeper place even if we don't fully understand it. The time to do this is whenever our life is asking it of us.

THE STILLNESS OF DESIRE

When we live in a state of desirelessness, we recognize that there is no "other" needed for our fulfillment. In a state of nonattachment, we realize our desires are superficial. They are only of the mind. This does not mean that if we are desireless we don't have anything, because in reality, when we truly desire nothing we have everything. Living in this state, there is never a question about wanting or not wanting something—only the reality of not needing it. We simply do not need anything in order to be free and complete.

It is only our attachment to things that binds and limits us. So often, we experience "I have this, it makes me happy. I don't have that, I feel unhappy." It's fine to be happy about having something, but the problem is that we are miserable without it. This pattern reinforces the belief that we cannot be happy without something other, and so we try to control life in order to get what we think will make us whole. When we believe there is something external that determines our experience, we start to blame something or somebody else for our unhappiness. We don't take responsibility for how we feel, and so we lose the power to change our experience. In this circular pattern, we thereby prove that "something" caused our misery.

If we buy into the idea that someone or something else can make us unhappy, we have just proved it to be true. We then continually reach outside ourselves to find whatever we think will fill the empty place in our own hearts. We feel this emptiness because of our perceived separation from God, but that perception is only a trick of the ego. If all of life is a manifestation of Pure Consciousness, how can we be separate from anything? When we are free from the misunderstanding that there is something missing in our life, we are also free from needing anything.

The mind is a trickster, and therefore we must transcend it. Stillness of desire comes from stillness of awareness and from subtle discrimination. When we are established in our center, our consciousness is always able to penetrate through the pain of not having or the pain of loss. Whatever we experience, we never lose contact with a level of fulfillment that is unconditional. I've said that desirelessness does not mean "not having" but rather "not holding." By repeatedly finding our center instead of living in our mind or emotions, we come to understand that it is only the attachment to something outside us that can cause us pain.

FREEING OURSELVES FROM ATTACHMENT

There is a profound difference between the need or desire for something, and simply celebrating having it. When we have what we want, and we could be enjoying its existence in our life, what do we usually do instead? We strangle it to death in our attempt to hold on to it. Fear of loss begins to surface, and that makes us contract. We are no longer concerned about what we were originally attached to, but simply unhappy about what might happen if we lose it. An incredible fear locks us down, and so a vicious loop reinforces itself. The desires of the ego perpetuate the ego, and all of our pain and attachments are symptoms of that ongoing drama.

Freeing ourselves from attachments necessitates that we make some conscious choices. It may require the discipline to let go of what is binding us; to let go of some "thing" we feel we must have or we are going to die. But what happens when we surrender the very thing we can't let go of? We experience spaciousness and freedom. We feel stronger. Perhaps we should write notes to ourselves and post them everywhere, so the next time something starts to grip us, we have a reminder of what is happening—which is that we're being given the opportunity to find freedom.

The loss of whatever we hold on to can actually be God's way of bestowing Grace and freedom on us. But the receiving of this gift is not always easy, and our stillness of desire will be tested. Circumstances that provide opportunities for us to grow and change will continually be put in front of us. The mind has an incredible power to convince us of its own perspective. Because we are so attached to our desires, it requires a great deal of strength, courage, discipline, and clarity to gain our freedom.

It is vital to recognize that desire and attachment come from the mind—and that the mind is able to create an extraordinary amount of delusion in us. When we find ourselves caught in turmoil, it is a strong clue that we need to get still. Instead of immediately reacting to the incessant need to do something, find something, or get rid of something, we rest in stillness. If we do that, whatever we are attached to will lose its grip.

Whenever we come face-to-face with a powerful desire, we can extract the energy from it. We have, in effect, extended our energy outside of us, so we need to pull it back inside. As we focus on freeing ourselves from the bondage of desire, what we are really doing is opening our heart to its infinite capacity, which is the natural result of drawing the energy back into our psychic mechanism. Understand that it is the bondage of desire that is a problem, not the desire itself. It's just that so few of us can separate the two.

When we are centered in our heart we are able to extend ourselves as far as we want—out into anything and anybody—and we won't create attachment or need out of the situation. We live in the state of flow, allowing our heart to project our life in front of us. From this place of openness, there is no mind needing to attach to something, and no emotion to contract us.

Desirelessness is freedom from the incessant thought and feeling that life has to be a certain way. It is the recognition of the perfection of our life at every moment. In this acceptance, what *can* we desire, except to allow Grace to unfold? This is not a concept. It is not theory. It should be and can be our experience that perfection is unfolding in our life at every moment. When we still our desires and awareness we cut the cords of attachment, which frees us to be immersed in our highest Self. We discover unconditional joy within ourselves not by manipulating, pushing, and shoving, not by trying to make life different, but by simply diving into the state of consciousness where perfection is crystal clear.

THE STILLNESS OF WILL

Ultimately, desirelessness shows itself as stillness of will—which is beyond the mere acceptance of God's will. It is the celebration of God's will as it expresses itself through us. The capacity to live in and from simplicity is fundamental to being able to free ourselves and to allow Divine Presence to reveal Itself. When we find the stillness of breath, awareness, desire, and will, we gain the ability to truly open our heart and feel the incredible Presence that lies within—always there, just waiting for us to tune in to It.

When we align our will with God's, devotion arises and sets us free. As Nityananda said, "As is your devotion, so is your liberation." He also said, "Devotion is not intended to eliminate difficulty." What an amazing statement. It means we are not living in God's will if we can only be devoted when life is the way we think it ought to be. Nityananda's words are so powerful because they cut through any illusion we may have that if we open our heart, every aspect of life will henceforth be perfect.

Until we open deep enough to feel the emergent quality of devotion to the God within, we remain devoted to ourselves. We bow at the altar of ego, selfishness, and desire. The real opportunity to know a profoundly different place in ourselves can only arise from an open heart. Our relationship to the Divine rests in the commitment we make—which is an expression of our love, gratitude, devotion, and surrender—no matter what surfaces in our lives. We trust the God within when He presents us with the perfect contraction, the perfect situation that requires us to get bigger inside and find our freedom.

We cannot want freedom one day and not want it the next. We cannot appreciate it when we have it but be unwilling to work to find it again when we have lost it. Devotion is an act of service to the God within who is trying to express His own freedom through us. If that is not yet your experience, start at the bottom of the ladder and learn to serve, to give, and to extend yourself. This is how we sacrifice our selfishness, laziness, and self-centeredness. It's how we really get in touch with what life is asking of us and move beyond any resistance to offering what is needed.

RISING TO MEET GOD'S GRACE

Nityananda said many important things, but perhaps one of the most beautiful is the simple expression, "The ocean is vast; the amount that you take from it is dependent on the size of the container you bring." The ocean of Consciousness is vast. How big can we open our heart to allow it in? That is really the question. We have the opportunity to receive the gift of Life itself. The Grace of the Divine has flowed through thousands of great saints, everywhere on earth, and through thousands of people who were never even recognized as saints. It is not a person we contact when we establish a connection with a saint but simply the universal state of Divine Presence that emanates from such an individual.

Liberation emerges from the descent of God's Grace and the ascension of the seeker's devotion. These two forces converge in stillness, allowing God in and allowing us out. In stillness we make contact with profound Grace, every moment of our lives. *Every* moment of our lives—not just some moments. God gave us the experience of life so we can find our Divinity. Being human should not negate our Divinity, just as being Divine does not negate our humanity. Of course, the problem is that we consistently get caught in the duality of human existence and think we are separate from God. We lose contact with Unity as we identify with the dynamics of daily life, with being happy or sad. These fluctuations are natural, but we mistakenly believe that there is duality in those seeming opposites. When we enter into the sky of the heart, individuated consciousness merges with the Divine, allowing for the dissolution of all dualistic misunderstanding.

When we consider the lives of great saints, we are filled with a sense of awe because we sense that our own spiritual development could bring us the same level of inner realization. I've discussed the progression of experience that happens in the course of our spiritual growth. This transformation of awareness begins with freeing ourselves from the grip of the ego. We recognize that the ego, in its attempt to maintain its perception of separation, will produce an endless array of drama in our lives—all of which keeps us trapped in our tensions and patterns. And so the first step is to redirect our attention inside, so that we do not continue to engage the drama. Established within, we can break our patterns and free ourselves from the dominance of the ego.

Once we have made this shift, we have the opportunity to really transform ourselves by dissolving the veils of duality, which are the true source of our unhappiness. We recognize the nature of those veils and gain the ability to penetrate through them. Once this separation has been dissolved, we become a living expression of the Divine. We have transcended duality and have merged into the Source of our existence. Established in that state, only God remains.

This is never a linear process, but from the moment we truly decide we want to live with God we will begin to free ourselves from the camouflage the ego creates to sustain its existence and its sense of separation. When we are able to move past that camouflage, we see the real place from which this smoke screen is projected, and begin to understand these subtle veils. Then we can just walk through them, as if through a thin curtain, and become a living expression of the Divine. In this lifetime, in this body, we can have that experience.

What is it that starts this progression of transformation? Grace. Of all the people on the face of the earth, why is it that one individual versus another all of a sudden wants to know God? Again, we can only call it Grace. The descent of Grace must be met with our devotion, and that only happens in the deep stillness of our heart. From this place, we free the innate consciousness within us, which unfolds as a living experience. The opening of our awareness takes time. We can touch the sky of the heart at any point, but the permanent immersion into this state comes with the maturation of our spiritual practice.

SUBTLE DISCRIMINATION REVEALS OUR ESSENCE

On one hand, we can describe the growth of consciousness in technical terms. We build the structure, open the *cakras*, feel the flow, and allow the *Kuṇḍalinī* energy to awaken. *Kuṇḍalinī* then rises through the *cakras*, piercing and dissolving the *granthi*, releasing and freeing the innate consciousness within us. But simply having this energy move through us is not enough. As our vital force begins to rise up into the heart-space, the four aspects of stillness must be there: the stillness of breath, the stillness of awareness, the stillness of desire, and the stillness of will. This is what allows higher consciousness to become our permanent experience, and enables us to express our inner awareness outwardly. Our consciousness matures on the field of stillness. The basis of developing stillness is subtle discrimination, desirelessness, and devotion. These are the elements we must cultivate in order to really experience a state of stillness.

Nityananda describes subtle discrimination as seeing the One in the many. It is the capacity to penetrate through all duality, all expressed dimensions of Oneness, until we have the perception that we are not separate from That. In other words, we develop the ability to tune through to the one Source from which the many arises—the Divine Presence that always is and ever will be right here, within everything that has manifested.

It is purely our misperception that there is a mountain of obstacles between us and God. The choice to live in the utter simplicity of God's love is the first thing we must bring to our spiritual endeavor. Then our practice is to get more deeply in contact with that love and less with the mountain of obstacles we have built in front of ourselves, which we perceive as a barrier to living in Divinity.

We must become a master at meditation in order to find that sweet essence, and this requires becoming a master of our consciousness instead of continuing to be a slave to our unconsciousness. When we focus our awareness back into its own Source, we are merging into That which we always were. We are dissolving the veils of duality. The glimpses we have of pure being, of stillness, accompanied by feelings of love or joy, are God's Grace showing us, "This is what it is like." Grace is giving us the experience of who we really are so that we will know our way home, even if we get lost. Then it's up to us to do the inner work to actually get there.

Each time we meditate we should have the intention of making contact with our deepest essence. By allowing that resonance to arise within us, it begins to penetrate into and inform our ordinary consciousness. And, with a lot of time and practice, we develop the subtle discrimination required to make our connection permanent. In the progression toward liberation, we encounter all the gymnastics of our mind and emotions. We have to penetrate through all that, deeply let go, and be willing to contact the true source of separation between us and Divine Presence.

As we move deeper into ourselves, we allow the veils of duality to softly relax and dissolve, so that Presence becomes evident. The deeper we can penetrate into Presence, and the longer we can stay there, the more transformative power releases from within us. The energy then rises, dissolving all barriers as it moves through every level within us, until it pervades every dimension of life in which we operate. Presence is then self-evident, and established in that place within we can deal with any troublesome aspects of our life. Immersion in God's heart does not eliminate difficulties, and it will not necessarily create what we envision as the perfect life, but it will always give us the perfect opportunity to free ourselves.

The fact that there are innumerable forms of camouflage, dimensions, and levels of existence does not contradict the reality that there is only one single Source of life. Multiplicity is simply an expression of Oneness. However, in the quest to recognize the One in the many, never make the mistake of thinking that multiplicity is not real. Some traditions may say that life is an illusion, but Tantric practices teach that if there is only One, how could any part of Its expression be unreal?

When we don't understand that there is one Source of all existence, multiplicity brings unhappiness. We unfortunately do forget that there is only Unity at the source of everything. We get caught in the grip of the ego and lose ourselves in multiplicity—in the form of our mind and emotions. We get stuck in that arena, fighting with something, and don't even recognize that this level is not the problem. The manifestation is the expression of our ego: anger, fear, envy, jealousy, and need are all just effects of the fundamental veils of duality.

SURRENDERING OUR UNHAPPINESS

So we look for the Source. Don't focus on the grip of the ego or the veils of duality. Looking for the Source is like shining a light into darkness. When we turn on the light, all of the darkness disappears, the ego loses its grip, and the veils do not obscure anymore. We step out of the boxing ring—where, in reality, we are our own opponent. As we become one-pointed and develop the capacity to be free of the many things that have bound and limited us, we are able to let go whenever overpowering thoughts or emotions arise. We recognize them for what they are.

One of Nityananda's basic precepts was, "Do not hesitate to surrender all that keeps you from Śiva." I love this, because he is not saying, "Do not hesitate to let go of *some* of the things that keep you from Śiva." We must surrender *everything* that is in the way, and it absolutely does not matter what it is that keeps us from living in God's heart. Yet isn't it amazing how tenaciously we hold on to the right to be miserable, to be human, to feel our emotions, and believe our thoughts? These are the very things that bring us profound misery—yet we would go all the way to the Supreme Court to defend our right to maintain our limitations.

We continually defend our need to cling to precisely those things that limit us. People often say, "Do not deny me my right to be unhappy—don't tell me I don't have emotions, that I am not full of fear." They are correct from their perspective, but understand that we also have the right to be free.

Seeing the One in the many enables us to penetrate through all the trips, all the drama, and all the pain we get caught up in. When we finally do this, we understand that all those obstacles are simply the reinforcement of our confusion about why we are unhappy, and why we don't live in unconditional joy.

When we surrender, we are consciously choosing what is most important to us, namely our right to be free. It's helpful to have a gigantic sense of humor so that we can have some objectivity about our stuff and just lay it down. As Rudi always said, "Your shit ain't special." Stop struggling to change that which cannot be changed. Anger is anger. Fear is fear. All our emotional and mental drama ceases to affect our experience of life when we simply change the place we live in.

CHOOSING WHAT DIMENSION WE LIVE IN

The part of us that lives in the grip of the ego will always be there. The profoundly simple choice is to not get caught in the turmoil but instead center our attention on living in God's heart and experiencing Divine radiance. Just like the hamsa bird, which has a powerful ability to extract essence, we all have the potential to see the highest. We do not have to live in the darkness of our emotions. Subtle discrimination is what enables us to separate the sweetness from the pain. Our lives encompass a multiplicity of dimensions of consciousness, and it is always our choice whether we focus on our limitations or live in the openness and stillness of our hearts in a state of causeless joy.

We do not need to analyze our limitations. Whenever we can move beyond our pain, fear, anger, or self-rejection by simply penetrating through it, we will feel its grip on us has dissolved. This is how we realize that something deeper is happening beneath the experience we thought we were having. We penetrate through the level of struggle—we stop identifying with our thoughts and emotions—and see that all of it was only the bonfire the ego had created in order to capture and hold our awareness in the most superficial dimension of life.

As we develop the capacity to move beyond our boundaries, we also gain the courage to live beyond our fears. It may hurt to let go of our limitations because we identify with them, thinking they are integral to who we are. But the pain of transformation is only a subset of the broader experience of opening up and residing in love and joy—and when we experience pain from this perspective it becomes insignificant. In order to function on a different level, what really must happen? First, through subtle discrimination, we tune in to a place of stillness inside. Then, we have to let go. We surrender and ask to be helped. This is what gives us the strength to open, choose joy, and move out of the problem. What we are really doing is obliterating our misunderstanding of who we think we are, transcending duality, and merging with God.

GOD IS ALWAYS HELPING US

There is only one thing happening in our lives: God is always trying to expand His own freedom through us. And despite the joy and freedom offered, we continually try to deny ourselves liberation by resisting God. So often we steadfastly refuse to open to the possibilities given to us because we label and judge a situation and think, "That's not for me. I shouldn't have to deal with that." But after we have gone through some major trauma, we might in retrospect feel that we really could have, or should have, surrendered more than we did. We have missed the opportunity, but it will come around again because God will continue to pursue the expansion of freedom.

This process of surrender is not different from what Nityananda prescribes when he says, "Look for the One in the many, look for the subtle in the gross." Subtle discrimination is an integral part of surrender because it allows us to get past our current level of experience, past wherever we feel stuck.

Everything is Divinely offered to us to free us of our separation. Something only hurts because we hold on to it. When we let go of it, where is the pain? I've said that our life is projected from the field of our consciousness onto the field of experience for the single purpose of setting up the obstacle course we must navigate to find our freedom. If we are caught in arguing about why the bar in front of us is four feet tall when we think it should only be three feet, we can get trapped there for lifetimes and we will have missed the point, which is to jump over it!

Isn't it amazing how often we forget about God when we are gripped by difficulty? One of the simplest ways out of our pain is to ask to be free of it, to ask God for help. But we must also realize that God is always helping us. This is what is really happening, and it is why we have to go through all our suffering, all this pain of transformation. The deepest place within us has asked for freedom, and life is presenting us with the perfect opportunities to grow. They may not fit the image of what we want in our lives, but they are what we need.

Only from the vantage point of stillness can we see, feel, and understand that our surface pain is just the manifestation of the deeper pain of separation. Knowing that a situation is not there to cause pain, we then have the ability not only to surrender and detach from whatever is going on, but to transform our own experience of life. Our capacity to recognize that God is always helping us is built on the foundation of stillness—the stillness of breath, awareness, desire, and will.

LIFE IS THE JOURNEY AS GOD

When we are completely open, all mind, thoughts, emotions, and desires simply dissolve. It is in devotion that we begin to live in God. I've quoted the Sufi adage, "It is not the journey to God, it is the journey in God." Tantric practices voice this as, "Life is the journey *as* God." We are aligning our will with God's, and the only expression of His will is liberation—the freedom to live in unconditional fulfillment and joy.

Traditionally, devotion has involved ritual performances. However, external practice, as it matures, should become an internal act of devotion, which has no form. In this sense, surrender is the greatest act of devotion, and it does not need bells, whistles, or *pūjās* to express itself. The simple act of bowing down or offering a flower can help us contact the highest surrender in ourselves, but what is unfortunate is that many people stop at the level of ritualistic devotion, of being devoted to some other. The most profound act of devotion is simply loving God and allowing His will to flow through us. In other words, devotion must mature into surrendering ourselves, which then leads to total immersion in God.

In this state there is no question of there being a devotee and an object of devotion. There is simply God being God, or, seen from another perspective, God being devoted to Himself. Established in stillness of will, we are an instrument of Divinity as It expresses Itself in and through our lives—not only for ourselves but for others. We exist for the very purpose of allowing God to be freer. This means more love, more absolute, unconditional joy, expanding to infinity. And where is the edge or the end of the infinite? There is none. Only we, by limiting our own experience, create a boundary.

The power of the ego has the same capacity to obscure reality as the Divine has to reveal it. For this reason, any person who moves close to Presence must always remain aware of the Source that brought them to a higher state of consciousness. It only takes a billionth of a second, a blinking of our attention, for us to lose contact and for the ego to proclaim, "This is me, I am the doer." This can even be true for great teachers. They feel the power of God within them, and it is very easy to forget whose power it is. Not forgetting the Source is the test of every teacher throughout time immemorial—and any teacher who thinks they have passed the test, just failed. So all one can do, student and teacher alike, is surrender and pray, "God, deliver me from myself."

Sometimes students ask, "What about being attached to the desire for liberation? Does this also need to be surrendered?" Our wish to grow is the one thing we should not surrender, because the fulfillment of that desire will bring unconditional joy and freedom. Through focusing on this highest desire we are uncovering a potential within us, rather than looking for something outside of ourselves. The desire to know that which is inherently within us is no desire at all. It is simply recognizing what already exists.

It is always important to clarify what we really want most in life—to ask ourselves some important questions. Are we sacrificing our own profound joy by holding on to the things that ultimately do not fulfill us? What are we willing to sacrifice for happiness? Conversely, are we willing to forgo living in a state of unconditional happiness because we are focused on the need to have something, do something, or to preserve our limited self-image?

My advice is to want God with all your heart. Want God so much it hurts. Want God so much you cry. If that is your wish, you can have everything else because you never forget what you really want. Living in stillness and surrendering to the will and Grace of God is the highest use of the life we have been given.

GOD IS LOOKING AT YOU . . . ARE YOU LOOKING BACK?

Grace is the highest gift from the Divine. It is the descent of the Divine, the perpetual unfolding of fullness that rains down upon each of us. There is nothing as miraculous as Grace—except our own conscious capacity to look back at God. We each have been endowed with Divine Consciousness, which includes the ability to respond to God as He is revealed within and around us.

What good is it if God is just looking at us? Except for the capacity to look back and say, "Yes, I see you," we are like tumbleweeds being blown aimlessly around the desert. How extraordinary that we are able to feel God's Grace upon us and allow It to transform our consciousness, transform our experience, and free us.

When we understand that we are alive because of Grace—and more importantly, that we are *experiencing* our life because of Grace—then we begin to shift our focus. We respond to Grace, rather than ignoring or rejecting It. We recognize and absorb Its power, a light that fills us and dissolves all limitation. Just as a flower opens and follows the sun, we can focus on God, allowing His light to lead us out of the darkness of our own misunderstanding, pain, and suffering. And when we experience this depth of transformation, our joy shows itself as unconditional gratitude and devotion.

In Tantric practices Divine Consciousness is defined as that which illuminates the light of life. As individuated, Self-aware expressions of the Divine, we are not separate from God's creative power, and so it is really *we* who are illuminating life. Tuning in to this illuminating consciousness and becoming aware of our own Self is the essence of *sādhana*, or practice. As the flowering of consciousness unfolds, the petals of our own experience become love, gratitude, devotion, surrender, stillness, and Presence.

When we find ourselves not having that experience, we must have the consciousness to ask ourselves why. Not having it, not living there, not pursuing it in the depths of our soul, is a choice we have made. Whatever it is that we perceive to be a barrier between us and God is only an obstacle if we allow it to remain so. Stop struggling with yourself and with your life; instead, transcend all limitations by burning them in the fire of consciousness.

Liberation comes through the descent of Grace and the ascension of the devotion of the seeker, and stillness is the place where those two forces converge. Centered there, we can hear God's voice because we are not filled with our own misunderstanding.

In stillness we can truly experience Divine Presence and allow Grace to penetrate into our depth and wash away our confusion. Grace is raining down upon us all the time. We have the choice to put up an umbrella so It cannot touch us—or to consciously walk out into the rain, strip ourselves of every defense, and allow God's lightning bolt to strike.

Let your liberation show itself. God is speaking to us every moment of our life, trying to show us His Grace. Be still and you can hear His voice. Allow the light of the Divine to illuminate your consciousness, and witness and recognize God's will and God's Grace creating your life. Who would want it any other way?

IF TRANSFORMATION AND LIBERATION
ARE WHAT YOU REALLY WANT,
OPEN YOUR HEART, FEEL THE FLOW,
AND SURRENDER EVERYTHING.

DO THAT WITH DEPTH OVER TIME
AND YOU WILL RECOGNIZE THAT
GOD DWELLS WITHIN YOU, AS YOURSELF.

PRONUNCIATION GUIDE

Trika tradition reflects the understanding that Sanskrit is a sacred, revealed language, its phonemes imbued with Śakti's power of manifestation. Sanskrit words are generally pronounced as in English, with some exceptions. Readers can use the key given here as a guide to proper pronunciation.

VOWELS

Sanskrit vowels are long or short. In English transliteration, long vowels are marked with a horizontal bar over the letter. The vowels "e" and "o" are always pronounced as long vowels.

ā	the long a, as in palm
e	as in wave
ī	the long i, as in deed
o	as in home
ū	the long u, as in pool

CONSONANTS

c	ch, as in chat
ṣ, ś	sh

TrikaShala & Rudramandir

Swami Khecaranatha is the spiritual leader of TrikaShala, the meditation program at Sacred Space Yoga Sanctuary, a nonprofit organization in Berkeley, California. TrikaShala teaches *Kuṇḍalinī sādhana* through classes, retreats, immersions, and engagement with a spiritual community. Weekly classes, which include *śaktipāta* transmission, are free of charge. For more information about attending your first *Kuṇḍalinī* class or retreat, please call (510) 486-8700 or visit *TrikaShala.com*.

TrikaShala is located in Rudramandir: A Center for Spirituality and Healing. Its mission is to serve the community by offering a breadth of programs to aid in the exploration of each individual's full potential. The experience of celebration and expansion at Rudramandir is enhanced through the adornment of the space with sacred art in the form of sculpture, painting, and architectural elements, evoking the magnificence of Spirit. Additional information is available at *Rudramandir.com*.

Recommended Reading

Dyczkowski, Mark S. G. *The Canon of the Saivagama and the Kubjika Tantras of the Western Tradition*

_____. *The Doctrine of Vibration*

_____. *A Journey in the World of the Tantras*

Dyczkowski, Mark S. G. and Vasugupta. *The Stanzas on Vibration*

Dyczkowski, Mark S. G. and Bhaskara. *The Aphorisms of Siva*

Hatengdi, M. U. *The Sky of the Heart: Jewels of Wisdom from Nityananda*

Hatengdi, M. U. and Swami Chetanananda. *Nityananda: In Divine Presence*

Mann, John. *Rudi: 14 Years With My Teacher*

Ridley, Charles. *Biodynamic Cranial Practice and the Evolution of Consciousness*

Swami Rudrananda. *Entering Infinity*

_____. *Rudi In His Own Words*

_____. *Spiritual Cannibalism*

Swami Shankarananda. *Consciousness Is Everything*

OTHER RESOURCES

Rudi: The Teachings of Swami Rudrananda
Available on DVD at *rudimovie.org*

Nityananda history: *Nityanand.org*

Nityananda history, stories, and sutras: *Nityananda.us*

Nityananda lineage: *NityanandaTradition.org*

Swami Rudrananda lineage: *RudranandaLineage.com*

PERMISSIONS